Bubble Monster

and Other

Science Fun

John H. Falk

Robert L.
Pruitt II

Kristi S.
Rosenberg

Tali A. Katz

CHICAGO
REVIEW
PRESS

Library of Congress Cataloging-in-Publication Data

Bubble monster and other science fun / John H. Falk . . . [et al.]. –
1st ed.
   p.   cm.
Includes bibliographical references.
ISBN 1-55652-301-7
1. Science–Experiments. 2. Science–Study and teaching–Activity programs. 3. Scientific
recreations. I. Falk, John H. (John Howard), 1948– .
Q164.B93   1996   96-8568
507.8–dc20   CIP

The author and the publisher of this book disclaim all liability incurred in connection with
the use of the information contained in this book.

Illustrations by Charles C. Somerville

First edition
Published by Chicago Review Press, Incorporated
814 North Franklin Street
Chicago, Illinois 60610
ISBN 1-55652-301-7
Printed in the United States of America

5 4 3

CONTENTS

Part One

How to Use This Book

Introduction

Blowing buckets of bubbles, stacking towers of blocks or boxes until they topple with a satisfying crash, building castles of graham crackers that you can gobble up when you're done—what could be more fun for children ages three to eight? *Bubble Monster* is packed with activities like these. Each one is wonderful fun, and, best of all, each teaches real science, the kind that is available to everybody as a basic part of our everyday world, if we only stopped to think about it.

The activities and stories in this book invite children and their caretakers to play and then to stop and think about one or more of five general science topics: patterns, matter, communication, the human body, and design and technology—wind, sound, water, and more. They were developed by the ScienceMinders project of the YWCA of Annapolis and Anne Arundel County with funding from the National Science Foundation with the goal of creating fun yet educational science activities that parents, teachers, daycare providers, and baby-sitters of all ages could do with young children. The activities were tested in elementary schools, daycare centers, homes, science centers, and YWCAs nationwide to be sure that they worked, that they taught basic science concepts, and that they were safe and lots of fun. None of the activities requires complicated materials, and all can easily be done at home, in the school yard, or in the classroom. They can be done in any order, and there are no right or wrong answers for any of them—just lots of questions that invite children and their caretakers to play, explore, laugh, and learn.

To get the most out of each activity, here are a few tips to keep in mind:

1. It's best to read the entire activity before doing it, but especially the "Read It" and "Think About It" sections.

3

2. If your child or children don't want to do the activity exactly as instructed, be flexible and let the children be creative. You may need to let them play before focusing on the steps suggested. That is perfectly OK.

3. Because every child is different, the age suggestions given for each activity should be thought of as just that–suggestions. They should be pretty accurate, though, most of the time.

4. Always make sure to match the activity to the child and the situation. Some children really like stories and others really like to build. Sometimes you need to quiet a child down, and other times you may want to do something active and exciting. Use your good judgment.

5. Always do the activity with the child. Don't be afraid to get down on your hands and knees and "Do It." This delights the child, and who knows–you, too, might learn some science and have some fun.

The Activity Index on page 17 will give you a quick guide to activity names, appropriate ages, science topics covered, and page numbers for easy reference. For more information on working and playing with young children, please read the Early Childhood Basics section that begins on page 10. We have also included a list of books and stories that children will love to hear on page 14 and a section on safety tips on page 16.

ABOUT THE SCIENCE TOPICS

Patterns

Everywhere we look in nature there are patterns–patterns in snowflakes and rocks, patterns in leaves and flowers, patterns in buildings and bridges. The "Spot the Patterns" activity emphasizes that patterns are everywhere. Animals depend upon recognizing patterns in order to find food, shelter, and mates. Humans, too, depend upon patterns for survival. We spend our lives searching for patterns in an attempt to understand the world around us. We use patterns to try to predict what the future will be like. For example, meteorologists try to predict the weather every day based on patterns of wind, sunlight, and temperature. The "Weather Patterns" activity will allow you to try your hand at predicting the weather. Understanding the way the world works makes things predictable and safe. Science and mathematics developed out of attempts to find patterns in nature.

Patterns is a topic area that overlaps with the other topic areas in this book. Patterns are needed to

Design and build things. Can you find the patterns in the "Graham Cracker Castles" activity? Patterns are used to understand the similarities and differences between the **Human Body** and the bodies of other animals. In "Animal Olympics" you can compare the abilities of a variety of other animals to those of humans. Patterns help us interpret the very small world of atomic and molecular **Matter**. The forces and organization of the atomic and molecular world give structure to the universe. The "Dress a Salad" activity, for example, encourages exploration of one aspect of this structure, the density of different materials. When we hear a sound, we interpret it as either noise or information. Noise is sound that, to our ears, has no pattern; information is sound that does have a recognizable pattern. This recognizable pattern is what enables the sound to become **Communication**. The "1-800-Cup-Talk" activity will allow you to discover the difference between noise and information.

All of this ability to find patterns in the world is made possible by our brains–the best pattern recognition instrument ever developed. In fact, the human brain is better than any computer ever designed at recognizing patterns. Our brain constantly receives signals from our senses and translates them into useful information about the world. This information is stored as memories, which in turn are used to help identify more patterns–patterns like the faces of family and friends or the letters on this page.

Matter

Matter pertains to the areas of chemistry and physics. Chemistry is the study of chemicals. Everything around us is made of chemicals; for example, food, houses, the sky, cars, and even our bodies. All of these things are composed of one, two, or hundreds of chemicals called elements. Elements are the building blocks of chemistry. By studying what things are made of and how they react  with other things, new and useful substances can be made. When chemicals are put together they produce reactions. There are chemical reactions occurring all the time. Flaming matches, rising cakes, and rusting cars are examples of reactions. Even our bodies have chemical reactions that occur constantly and are fueled by the addition of the food we eat and the oxygen we breathe.

Through the use of chemical experiments performed in laboratories, chemists have already produced medicines, plastics, adhesives, paints, and even gas, to list a few. Chemists try to sort everything into groups. Chemicals can be divided into solids, liquids, and gases or into metals and nonmetals.

Physics is the study of all the things around us and the energy they possess. The world we live in is full of energy. Light, heat, sound, motion, magnetism, and electricity are some of the forms that energy takes.

Light travels in waves and we see it when it reflects off of objects or travels through them. Heat is another form of energy that is created when molecules vibrate, passing energy from one to another. The "Slip and Slide" activity demonstrates this concept. Sound is another form of energy that travels in waves. All sounds occur because something, like your vocal chords, vibrates, which in turn makes molecules in the air vibrate. The vibrating air molecules make our eardrums vibrate, which results in nerve impulses to our brain, which results in us hearing sound. The activity "1-800-Cup-Talk" is designed to allow experimentation with sound waves. Physicists call the things that make objects move, stop, change direction, or change shape *forces*. A force that everyone on Earth is familiar with is gravity. Gravity is a force that pulls down on every single thing on Earth. What forces besides gravity might be at work in the "Totally Tubular" and "Hard Headed" activities?

Scientific understanding of these various forms of matter and energy have resulted in the invention of most of the things we consider fundamental to modern life–things like telephones, automobiles, modern cosmetics, computers, television, radios, compact disc players, modern medicines, and refrigerators, just to name a few.

Communication

All living things communicate at some level. Some social animals like monkeys and crows spend much of the day involved in communicating, while some animals, like simple one-celled organisms, communicate very little. Communication is one of the basic properties of life. We usually think of communication as being from one person to another, but communication can also be from some other type of living thing to another. For example, when we see a bee fly by, its yellow and black stripes are communicating "beware." Some plants and animals try to mask how much they communicate. This is the idea being presented in "Betcha Can't Find It!"; camouflage is a kind of reverse communication. Some biologists spend all their time studying animal communication, sometimes because the things learned from animal communication help us better understand human communication. Do you think "Animal Cracker I.D." could help you be a better human communicator?

To be human is to need to communicate. We communicate through spoken language, through written language, and through nonverbal means such as the raising of an eyebrow, a smile, or our posture. Much of human communication is so fundamental to our humanness that we don't even think about it. Social scientists like psychologists, linguists, sociologists, and anthropologists study human communication. One way humans have learned to communicate is through colors, for example traffic signals. The "A-Maze-N Colors" activity teaches about communication through colors by forcing us to learn new meanings for old colors.

The basics of communication are pretty simple. Some form of energy, be it light, pressure, or sound, must be transmitted. For that transmission of energy to become "communication," the energy "transmitter" and the energy "receiver" must both recognize the same patterns. In other words, if I speak to you, you must recognize the sounds you hear as speech in order for communication to have occurred. If my speech sounds to you like so much noise, that is not communication. The basic challenge of communication is to share information with clarity–a maximum amount of information with a minimum amount of noise. This is the challenge that communication scientists have worked on perfecting for years while developing such wondrous communication inventions as the telephone, television, radio, and new computer-assisted communication like the Internet. Human communication technology has come a long way from the days of smoke signals and "talking" drums.

The Human Body

The human body is a wondrous thing. Composed of billions of individual cells linked together in interacting systems of organs, the human body is able to move, reproduce, grow, learn, fight off disease, breathe, and energize itself, all without us having to think about it. The product of millions of years of evolution, the human body is very, very good at doing things that we take for granted. For example, without a lot of thought and without even having to see, our nose and brain are able to tell us whether someone is cooking bacon and eggs or pancakes for breakfast. As can be discovered in "The Nosy Detective," our sense of smell is remarkably well developed, as are our senses of touch, sight, hearing, and taste. Scientists recently discovered that humans have more than one thousand different types of smell receptors in the brain, each receptor tuned to a different smell.

For young children, one of the most miraculous aspects of the human body is the coordination of muscles, bones, and nerves that permits us to run, jump, skip, hop, pick up things, and put them down again. Several activities highlight these large motor skills— "Busy Bodies," "Animal Olympics," "Muscle Madness," and "Fantastic Finger Feats." Our body contains dozens of movable parts. Each part is given structural strength by bones; each bone is controlled by pairs of muscles; each muscle is, in turn, controlled by networks of nerves running between the muscles and the brain. Each part of the system is designed to do one very small task, but in combination, the parts permit our bodies to perform remarkably complex movements. Medical doctors and scientists who study human physiology have been studying how the bones and muscles work together; their work is helping not only those with problems, but is also leading to enhanced performances by athletes and dancers.

The control center for the whole system is the brain. The brain receives signals from all parts of the body. All of our internal systems are continuously monitored by the brain, even when we are sleeping. Information coming from the outside world, like light and sound, are combined with information from inside our body, like feelings and hunger, to create our perceptions of the world. When the internal world gets shaky, such as happens when we're dizzy, our view of the external world also gets shaky. Try doing the "Total Dizziness" activity and learn firsthand how changes in our internal state can directly affect our view of the external world. Greater understanding about the interrelationships between the brain and the body are leading to better techniques for curing disease and may even lead to improved techniques for helping children learn.

Design and Technology

Technology extends our abilities to change the world. It allows us to cut, shape, or put materials together; to move things around; and to communicate better with our hands, voices, and senses. We use technology to try to change the world to suit us better.

The changes may relate to survival needs such as food, shelter, or defense, or they may relate to human aspirations such as art. Because the world is unpredictable, technology and design are affected by costs, side effects, and risks.

Design often involves great creativity in inventing new approaches to challenges and great innovation in seeing new challenges or new possibilities. Constraints placed on design present challenges that make it impossible to construct a perfect design. Some constraints are cost, public opposition, disruption of the natural environment, and disadvantages to some people, to name just a few.

Designs always require testing. Testing is often done by using small-scale physical models, computer simulations, or analysis of systems that replace other systems (for example, laboratory animals stand in for humans). If you were planning to construct a large-scale building, you would first want to construct a small-scale physical model. Architects regularly make small models of their buildings before building the large, real thing; so, too, do bridge and road engineers. Designers, whether exhibit, clothing, automobile, or toy, build prototypes, which are full-scale models of the final product. Think of "Graham Cracker Castles" as an activity about building models. The model or prototype can be used to test a variety of ideas such as the materials needed, general appearance, possible costs, and perhaps even the effect on the environment.

When considering any new technology there are some key questions that should be asked. For example, What are alternative ways to accomplish the same goals? Who will suffer or benefit as a result of the proposed new technology? What will the proposed new technology cost to build and operate? What risks are associated with the proposed new technology? What people, materials, tools, knowledge, and know-how will be needed to build, install, and operate the proposed new technology? What will happen when the new technology becomes obsolete or worn out? How will it be replaced? Though these questions sound complex, do not be fooled; even the simplest designs require many of these same questions to be answered. For example, the "Stacks of Fun" activity asks you to construct towers in your home. In order to accomplish this you will need to ask and have answers to some of these questions. What types of building materials will be needed? Will there be any cost? How many people are needed to build the towers? How can a newer and better tower be constructed using new technology or building materials?

Not all of the questions can be answered immediately. Most decisions will be made on the basis of incomplete information. But scientists, mathematicians, architects, designers, and engineers have the job of trying to accurately estimate the benefits, side effects, and risks of creating new technologies and products.

EARLY CHILDHOOD BASICS

The activities in this book are designed with the young child in mind. However, young children will most likely not purchase this or any other book without assistance from a parent, older sibling, or baby-sitter. It is you, the primary caregiver, to whom we want to speak to at this time. We want you to enjoy this book and get the most out of each activity that you select.

In talking to parents, early childhood professionals, and baby-sitters we were encouraged by their willingness to continue learning more about the growth and development of children in an attempt to better relate to and work with them. To ensure greater success using this book, we wanted to equip you with some growth and development information as it relates to the activities in this book.

Each activity lists a suggested age. The suggested age corresponds to a child's ability to perform the steps in the "Do It" sections of the activities. When proper activities are selected they will be child-directed and adult-facilitated. It is our hope that the child will be able to perform the majority of the steps with little assistance. We will say more about the role of the facilitator later. Selecting activities requires some knowledge regarding the abilities of children at different stages in their growth and skill development. Included in this book is a chart of ages and typical skills acquired at various stages in a child's development. Obtaining a better understanding of the capabilities of children between the ages of three and seven will ensure that you select activities appropriate for both the age and skill level of your child. Keep in mind that there is a significant amount of development that occurs during these years and the abilities and skills of three-year-olds are not the same as those of eight-year-olds. For example, your child is three and you select an activity with a suggested age of five. You feel that your child will enjoy the activity, but it calls for cutting and pasting. A three-year-old's skills generally do not include the ability to accomplish the task of cutting; recognizing this, you need to perform this task for the child. However, the child can paste and should always be encouraged to use the skills she possesses. This will support the development and strengthening of her skills, and it will afford her opportunities to actively participate in the experience. Involving the child provides her with a sense of accomplishment. Utilizing the chart and using the suggested ages for each activity will allow you to identify steps that the child can perform and those that will require greater assistance.

For those children possessing skills that exceed their age and require more of a challenge, we suggest that you utilize one or more of the following options:

1. Select an activity targeted for older children to increase the challenge for a younger child.

2. Refer to the challenge located in the "Try It" section of each activity. The challenge is designed to increase the skill level without altering the age that the activity calls for. The challenge can be done immediately following the activity or used as an independent activity.

3. Modify the activity so it will meet the needs of your child. The additional activities in the "Try It" section can be used to meet this demand or they can remain adjuncts to the original activity.

4. You may wish to use the activities as outlined and incorporate additional resources as a means of providing a greater challenge for your child.

Regardless of the method chosen, try the activity as written. Your child may gain some enjoyment from doing the activity with you.

Your role as a facilitator is a difficult one because it requires that you assist rather than lead the activity. Aside from merely gathering materials and setting up, you can and should do the activity. For instance, if an activity requires the child to draw a picture, draw your own picture rather than instructing the child on how his picture should look. Gaining a better understanding of this role will come with practice and will be defined in part by the child's needs; be patient with yourself. Reading the activities in advance will help you think of ways to get both you and the child actively involved in the activities. Children are naturally curious, active learners who will follow the lead of someone they trust–like you. So, it really should not take a lot for you to set up the activity and quickly explain what the child is to do. For example, "Betcha Can't Find It!" is an activity that requires the child to color a fish and create a background that matches the fish in an attempt to camouflage it. Once you complete the set-up, simply say, "Color the paper so it matches the fish." This may be a sufficient challenge for a three-, four-, or five-year-old. However, a seven-year-old may need a bigger challenge. "I challenge you to color your fish and create a background that will hide, conceal, or camouflage the fish so that it cannot be seen." Seek ways to creatively encourage your child to accept the challenge. Using the challenge located under each activity title is encouraged.

In addition, you should never suggest that the outcome of an activity is incorrect. These activities are designed for the child to have fun and promote thinking, which is the catalyst for discovery and learning. Discouraging words coupled with excessive control inhibit thinking and stifle creativity rather than promote them. Let the child work, think, discover, and learn at her own pace. Allow the child to explore different paths without becoming discouraged if the activity does not go as planned. After all, children bring their own experiences to the activity and these experiences can alter the expected result. If the child doesn't want to participate, simply go with the flow. Spend time doing what she wants to do and, more likely than not, she will eventually want to try the activity.

Give considerable thought to the importance of telling the child that the activities are science related prior to doing the activity. Your child may not recognize or make the connection between the activities used and science. In a formal educational setting you may want to explain to your child that he will be working with science materials. However, in an informal setting, we suggest that you wait until the conclusion of the activity to introduce the science information. We do not suggest this in an attempt to conceal the importance of science. Our experience shows that many children harbor negative notions regarding science, and thus shy away from science. If your family sets a time to play together, use this book for fun-time activities. Keep in mind that whenever these materials are used the child will have exposure to science. Learning takes time, and you never know, your child just may surprise you and make the connection between the activities and science concepts.

We hope this information has been and will continue to be helpful as you make your journey through the activities. We encourage you to occasionally refer to the developmental chart as a refresher—regardless of your experience working with children. In addition, we hope that you will enjoy your role as a facilitator. Keep in mind that the more you know about your child the better you will become at selecting activities and materials that are both age and developmentally appropriate. Have fun teaching as well as learning from your child. Let your child's imagination run free; encourage her to explore multiple paths in an attempt to arrive at her own conclusions regarding each activity.

Everyone who uses this book can have fun with science regardless of gender, ethnicity, and socioeconomic position. The notion that science can be fun seems to be overlooked in many classrooms and households, where the emphasis has been placed on rote learning and not on divergent thinking. The activities in this book promote thought while at the same time promoting fun and family interaction. Always remember, we as caregivers can only facilitate learning. Learning is controlled by the learner and will occur in its own time and at its own pace.

Early Childhood Skills Chart

Ages 3 to 5 years	Physical Abilities	Intellectual Abilities	Social and Emotional Abilities
	−can throw objects and begin to catch −likes to climb and run −can string beads and build towers with blocks −can feed self but often spills −likes to paint and play with clay −climbs stairs easily, hops, and skips −dresses self but sometimes needs help with zippers and snaps −enjoys puzzles, lacing-type toys, and crayons −is learning to copy designs, letters, and numbers	−can follow simple instructions −knows more than she can express −has an attention span of about 10 to 20 minutes −uses three- to four-word sentences −recognizes some shapes and colors −has difficulty with abstract concepts, such as time −is very curious and asks many questions −imitates others and likes dramatic play −begins to distinguish between fantasy and reality −likes music, rhythm, and stories	−likes to imitate adult actions and wants to help with chores −can tidy up toys −is still possessive but is learning to share −seeks approval from adults −can ask for help when she needs it −can be bossy and at other times protective of younger children −has a sense of pride for her belongings and accomplishments
Ages 6 to 8 years	Physical Abilities	Intellectual Abilities	Social and Emotional Abilities
	−plays actively with children his own age −enjoys running games, such as tag, dodge ball, skipping, and more −is capable of using tools and scissors with ease −is becoming more coordinated −can throw and catch well	−is learning to read and grasp basic math concepts −can plan ahead and solve problems −likes to play with peers and can play cooperatively −is improving vocabulary and ability to use language to explain his emotions −shows greater interest in reality and less in fantasy play −has a greater attention span—20 plus minutes	−likes group activities and team games −can accept more responsibility −enjoys a challenge −likes praise and seeks approval from adults and peers −is learning to control his fears *Source: Taken from Home Child Care, Caregiver's Guide (Dunster, 1994).*

SUGGESTED READING

I. Suggested books under the topic of Communication:

1. Mendoza, George, *Traffic Jam* (Stewart, Tabori & Chang, 1990)

2. Cummings, Pat, *Jimmy Lee Did It* (Lothrop, Lee & Shepard, 1985)

3. Martin, Bill, and John Archambault, *Listen to the Rain* (Henry Holt & Company, 1988)

4. Most, Bernard, *Can You Find It?* (Harcourt Brace & Company, 1993)

5. Ahlberg, Janet and Allen Ahlberg, *Each Peach Pear Plum* (Penguin Group, 1978)

6. Brown, Margaret Wise, *Red Light, Green Light* (Scholastic Inc., 1992)

7. Blanchard, Arlene, *Sounds My Feet Make* (Random House, 1988)

8. Bourke, Linda, *Eye Spy* (Chronicle Books, 1991)

9. Stilwell, Stella, *Animal Colors* (Barron's, 1991)

10. Young, Ed, *Seven Blind Mice* (The Putnam & Grosset Book Group, 1992)

11. Hayes, Sarah, *Eat Up* (Lothrop, Lee & Shepard, 1988)

II. Suggested books under the topic of Matter:

1. Sadler, Marilyn, *Alistair Underwater* (Simon & Schuster, 1988)

2. Stafford, William, *The Animal That Drank Up Sound* (Harcourt Brace Jovanovich, 1992)

3. Wisniewski, David, *Rain Player* (Clarion Books, 1991)

III. Suggested books under the topic of Patterns:

1. Rikys, Bodel, *Red Bear's Fun with Shapes* (Penguin Books, 1993)

2. McMillan, Bruce, *Eating Fractions* (Scholastic Inc., 1991)

3. Oakes, Bill and Suse MacDonald, *Puzzlers* (Penguin Books, 1989)

4. Oakes, Bill and Suse MacDonald, *Numblers* (Penguin Books, 1988)

5. Hoban, Tana, *Shapes and Things* (Macmillan, 1970)

IV. Suggested books under the topic of the Human Body:

1. Martin, Bill, and John Archambault, *Here Are My Hands* (Henry Holt and Company, 1987)
2. Ferber, Elizabeth, *Once I Was Very Small* (Annick Press, 1993)
3. Stevenson, James, *The Mud Flat Olympics* (Greenwillow Books, 1994)

V. Suggested books under the topic of Design and Technology:

1. Domanska, Janina, *I Saw a Ship A-Sailing* (Macmillan, 1972)
2. Radford, Derek, *Harry Builds a House* (Macmillan, 1990)
3. Crews, Donald, *Harbor* (Greenwillow, 1982)
4. Nolan, Dennis, *The Castle Builder* (Macmillan, 1987)
5. Neville, Emily C., *The Bridge* (Harper & Row, 1988)
6. Pfanner, Louise, *Louise Builds a Boat* (Orchard, 1990)
7. Sadler, Marilyn, *Alistair in Outer Space* (Hamish Hamilton, 1984)
8. Williams, Vera B., *A Chair for My Mother* (Greenwillow, 1982)
9. Huchins, Pat, *Changes, Changes* (Macmillan, 1971)

SAFETY TIPS FOR MINOR MISHAPS

While it is unlikely that you will ever face an emergency situation while caring for children, it is a good idea to think about what you will do if a problem occurs. Most of the everyday accidents that children experience are not very serious. However, if more than a hug and a kiss are needed to make it all better, be sure to inform the parents. Even the smallest bump can turn into a bruise that will surely alarm any parent.

We have provided you with a chart of some common mishaps and suggestions for administering first aid. We recommend that you obtain more safety and emergency information from your local YWCA, library, or police station. Be sure to get pamphlets on what to do in case of the following: fire, poison, medical emergencies, drowning, choking, electric shock, burns, and unconsciousness or trauma, to list just a few. The more information that you have the better prepared you will be. Keep your pamphlets with you at all times. Furthermore, make a copy of the chart and keep it with you at all times or post a copy next to the phone.

Safety Chart

Mishaps	Suggested Action
Bumps and Bruises	Place an ice pack or ice wrapped in a clean towel on the affected area for up to 10 minutes for every hour period until the swelling decreases.
Abrasions (skinned knees and elbows)	Wash your hands and clean the area with a washcloth, soap, and warm water. Pat dry with a clean towel. Leave abrasion exposed to heal faster. A bandage can be used to prevent clothes from rubbing. Do not put any medicine on the abrasion.
Cuts	Wash your hands, clean the cut with a clean washcloth, soap, and warm water, and cover with a bandage. If there is a lot of bleeding, press a cloth against the cut until the bleeding stops. Cover with a bandage. If the cut is large and/or deep and you can't stop the bleeding then call a doctor or 911.
Puncture Wounds (caused by pins or pointed objects)	Wash your hands, clean the area with a clean washcloth, soap, and warm water, and leave uncovered. If the puncture was due to an object like a nail, then contact parents and ask about a recent tetanus shot.
Nosebleeds (due to a fall, sneezing, or a cold)	Have the child sit forward and open her mouth while you gently pinch her nose closed with a clean cloth. Do this for about 10 to 15 minutes.
Splinters	Wash your hands and clean a pair of tweezers with soap and hot water or rubbing alcohol. If the splinter is sticking out, remove it with the tweezers. If the splinter is embedded, leave it in, clean the area with soap and water, and tell the parents when they return.
Swallowing Small Objects (marbles, buttons, or coins)	If the object is not stuck in the child's throat, do not be alarmed. Remove all other small objects from the play area. If the object is stuck and the child is choking, call 911 immediately and then call the child's parents. If the child stops breathing, let 911 know and they will give you further instructions.
Falls	If a young child falls and begins to cry or an older child gets the wind knocked out of him, don't worry. Comfort the child for a few minutes and encourage him to resume play. If the child is unable to sustain his balance, vomits, or has a hard time breathing, call the parents, doctor, or 911 immediately.

Source: Taken from The New Complete Babysitter's Handbook. *(Clarion Books, 1995).*

Activity Index

Age	Activity	Page Number	Communication	Design and Technology	Patterns	Matter	Human Body
3 to 5	Animal Cracker I.D.	25	X				X
3 to 5	Parade of Patterns	105			X		
3 to 5	Peek-a-Boo Picture	108	X		X		
3 to 5	Stretch It Out	133				X	
3 to 5	Taster's Choice	137				X	X
3 to 5	**Where Do I Go?**	**159**			X		
3 to 6	The Nosy Detective	99	X				X
3 to 7	Sounds Funny	123	X				X
3 and Up	Betcha Can't Find It!	38	X		X		
3 and Up	Bubble Monster	49			X	X	
3 and Up	Color Dance	59			X	X	
3 and Up	Edible Bridge	71		X		X	
3 and Up	Spot the Patterns	126			X		
3 and Up	Wave Maker	152				X	
4 to 6	Blown Away	42				X	
4 to 6	Driver's Test	68	X	X			
4 to 7	Fantastic Finger Feats	77					X
4 to 7	Hard Headed	87		X		X	X
4 to 7	Slip and Slide	120				X	
4 to 8	That's Attractive	140				X	
4 and Up	Help, We Need a Bridge!	90		X			
4 and Up	1-800-Cup-Talk	102	X	X		X	
5 to 7	Keep Your Balance	93					X
5 to 8	Graham Cracker Castles	81		X			
5 and Up	Animal Olympics	28					X
5 and Up	The Bat That Couldn't See	31	X			X	
5 and Up	Echo-o-o-e-e-s	35	X			X	X
5 and Up	Bricklayer	45			X		
5 and Up	Build a Better Chair	52		X		X	
5 and Up	Busy Bodies	55					X
5 and Up	Dinnertime	62	X				
5 and Up	Dress a Salad	65				X	
5 and Up	The Great Shoe Detective	84					X
5 and Up	Muscle Madness	96					X
5 and Up	My Personal Space Station	114		X			
5 and Up	Shelly's Space Adventure	111	X	X		X	
5 and Up	Stacks of Fun	130		X		X	
5 and Up	Total Dizziness	143					X
5 and Up	Weather Patterns	155			X		

Age	Activity	Page Number	Communication	Design and Technology	Patterns	Matter	Human Body
5 and Up	Zany Patterns	161		X	X		
6 and Up	Eye Need a Hand	74	X				X
6 and Up	Ships Ahoy	117		X		X	
7 and Up	A-Maze-N Colors	21	X				
7 and Up	Total Recall	146					X
7 and Up	Totally Tubular	149		X		X	

Part Two

The Activities

Age: 7 and Up
Time: 10 to 20 minutes

A-Maze-N Colors

A-MAZE-ING!

Can you walk through a maze using colors as a guide?

 ## Get it

 ## Read it

**Construction paper (21 orange
sheets, 11 green, 8 red, and 2 white)**
**Maze diagrams (provided on page
24)**
Index card
Markers (yellow, green, and red)

✓ *If you want to try this activity with children
young than age seven, we suggest you tape a
green band to their left wrist and a red band to
their right wrist. Even children above age seven
might benefit from having the directions written on
an index card.*

✓ *Make an "enter" and an "exit" sign on the sheets
of white paper. You will need this for your maze.*

✓ *You can use all white paper instead of the construction paper. But you will need to mark the
white paper with orange, green, and red stripes to
match the total number of orange, green, and red
sheets of construction paper listed above.*

Do it

1. Using the maze diagrams provided, ask the child to help you gather the colors needed for maze number one. Place the colors in order on the floor so they match maze number one.

2. Ask the child to take off her shoes and stand on the enter sign. Make sure that she understands which colors mean left, right, and straight ahead. Explain that each color will lead her to another color and then to the exit.

3. Explain that when the color says turn left or right the child must turn her body in that direction first and then step to the next color. If she makes a mistake, ask her to start at the beginning.

4. Ask the child to help you set up maze number two using the drawing as a guide. Take turns walking through the maze. Which maze was easier to walk through?

5. Create the third maze with the child out of the room. Ask the child to return and find her way through the maze. Do you see any similarities between the first and third mazes?

Try it

Make a travel version. Copy the mazes or create new ones on index cards. Use a coin or small toy as a marker that can be moved through the maze.

Walk back through the mazes starting at the exit. Remember to reverse the meanings of the colors.

Do the "Driver's Test" activity.

The A-Maze-N Challenge. Create your own 20-square maze with one or more entrances and exits. Take your time; it's harder than you think.

Think about it

In order for you to walk through the mazes you needed some information. You needed to know what the colors were asking you to do. Once you understood that the colors were communicating directions to you, you were able to start your journey. You may have encountered a few problems in the beginning because you did not always remember the direction assigned to each color. You were familiar with red meaning stop or danger, yellow meaning caution, and green meaning go. The colors were given different meanings and it took time to understand the new meanings. Once you understood the colors' meanings, the communication became understandable.

Maze #1

RED	RED	GREEN	GREEN
ORANGE	ORANGE	ORANGE	ORANGE
ORANGE	ORANGE	ORANGE	ORANGE
ORANGE	GREEN	ORANGE	GREEN
RED	ORANGE	ORANGE	GREEN

EXIT   ENTER

Maze #2

				ENTER
GREEN	ORANGE	ORANGE	ORANGE	
GREEN	ORANGE	ORANGE	RED	
GREEN	GREEN	GREEN	RED	
ORANGE	ORANGE	GREEN	RED	
ORANGE	RED	ORANGE	RED	

EXIT

Maze #3

ENTER		EXIT	ENTER
RED	RED	GREEN	GREEN
ORANGE	ORANGE	ORANGE	ORANGE
ORANGE	ORANGE	ORANGE	ORANGE
ORANGE	GREEN	ORANGE	GREEN
RED	ORANGE	ORANGE	GREEN

EXIT (left side)

ENTER   EXIT   ENTER

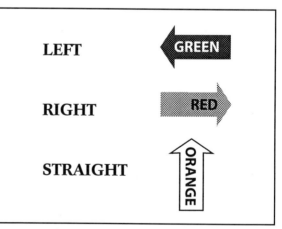

LEFT   GREEN

RIGHT   RED

STRAIGHT   ORANGE

Make bands to wear on wrists

Age: 3 to 5
Time: 10 to 20 minutes

Animal Cracker I.D.

Can you tell what an animal is by how it moves and sounds?

Get it

Box or bag of animal crackers
A bowl

Read it

✓ *Wash your hands before playing!*

✓ *Help the child practice making sounds and movements for each animal in the box.*

✓ *If the child is having difficulty identifying the animals, give him hints about where the animal lives or what it eats.*

✓ *Make sure the child chews and swallows each cracker before making other animal sounds or movements.*

Do it

1. Ask the child to pour the box of crackers into a bowl. Pick a cracker and hide it in your hand, making sure you know which animal you've chosen. Make noises and movements like the animal you have chosen. If the child correctly identifies the animal, he gets to eat the animal cracker! Now, take turns.

2. Try to identify at least four different animals. If you and the child pick the same animal then use different sounds and movements to describe your animal. How many animals was he able to i.d.? Were you able to make different sounds to represent the same animal?

3. Make animal sounds and movements like one of the animal crackers, for example a monkey. Now, ask the child to pick the animal out of the bowl that matches the sounds and the movements you have displayed. Take turns making the sounds and movements. How many animals was he able to i.d.?

4. Each of you pick a cracker and combine the sound of one animal with the movement of the other. For example, roar like a lion and walk like a monkey. Ask the child to identify both animals. Take turns trying to identify each other's animal.

BARK
BARK
BARK

ROAR!

GOT IT...

Try it

Select an animal cracker and create a short story about where that animal lives, what it eats, and what it looks like. Act out the story while the child guesses the animal that you are portraying.

Take a trip to the zoo. Compare your sounds and movements to those of the real animals.

Do the "Echo-o-o-e-e-s" and "Animal Olympics" activities.

The Animal Cracker Challenge. Combine the names of two animal crackers. For example, combine a lion and a monkey and get a lionkey (lie-on-key)! Now, tell the child that you are a lionkey. Have him look for the two animal crackers that make up that name.

Think about it

When you used animal sounds and movements you communicated or told people what kind of animal you were. Your sounds and movements gave the people guessing the information they needed to identify your animal. Animals use sounds and movements to locate each other, send warning signals, and scare something away. All animals have to learn what each sound and movement means. And even if two different animals have similar sounds and movements, their meanings may be very different. It is important for animals and humans to understand the meanings of sounds and movements in their environment. Obtaining this understanding of our world will allow us to communicate better with those around us.

Age: 5 and Up
Time: 10 to 20 minutes

Animal Olympics

Can you outjump a frog, outhop a kangaroo, outrun a cheetah, and carry things like an elephant?

 ## Get it

Pencil
Ruler or tape measure
7 coins
2 books
3 pillows

 ## Read it

✓ This activity is great for indoors or outdoors.
✓ Clear a big space if you're playing inside.
✓ Give the child a homemade Olympic medal as a reward for playing.
✓ You may want to keep a record of each event. This can be displayed on the kitchen refrigerator and can be used later to compare the child's progress.

Do it

1. The first event is the Frog Jump. Place a pencil in a horizontal position on the ground. Use your ruler

   or tape measure to mark off four feet from the pencil. Have the child place a coin on the floor every 12 inches. Ask the child to leap to the first coin. Have her return to the starting line and try jumping to the second, third, and fourth coins. Add more coins if the child jumps past the last coin. Record the number of coins that the child jumped past.

2. The second event is the Kangaroo Hop. Tell the child that kangaroos can hop high, fast, and for a long time. First, ask the child to hop for as long as she can when you say go. Then, ask her to hop as high in the air as she can three times. Finally, ask her to hop as many times as possible in 10 seconds. Record her times, heights, and repetitions.

BOING
BOING

3. The third event is the Cheetah Chase. Place two books on the ground at least 10 feet apart. Ask the child to pretend that both of you are cheetahs and can run very fast. To start the race, get down on all fours and place your hands beside one book. Say "go" and run up to and around the second book and back to the first book. Which one of you can win two races in a row?

READY? SET!

4. The final event is the Elephant Carry. Tell the child that elephants are strong animals that lift things with their trunks. Place three pillows on one side of the room and ask the child to stand at the opposite side of the room. Ask the child to hold one arm behind her back, run over to the pillows and pick up as many pillows as possible using her free arm like an elephant's trunk.

OKAY, NOW TRY 3...

Try it

Make masks for each of the animals. Wear them while you play the games.

The Animal Olympics Challenge.

Create a bird event, bunny hop race, crab walk, snake slither, and turtle crawl. You will have to decide what bird you want to imitate and what each race will look like. Make up your own rules and try them out.

Think about it

PERFORMANCE

Animals have evolved a variety of ways to avoid enemies and/or catch food. Some animals hop, some run, and some slither. Each strategy has proven successful, and each has its advantages and disadvantages. Humans cannot run as fast as cheetahs, hop as well as kangaroos or frogs, or even slither as fast as snakes. Our main strategy for escaping enemies or capturing food is to use our brains.

The Bat That Couldn't See

Can you imagine flying and using only your voice to guide you?

nce upon a time there lived a bat named Cody who had a problem. She had a hard time seeing things directly in front of her. Cody lived in a dimly lit attic with her parents.

Every night her friend Buggy would fly through a vent just above the attic window. He and Cody would hang upside down from the ceiling beams and talk for hours. "Hey Cody," Buggy shouted while scooting closer to Cody, "will you fly with me tonight?"

"No, you go on without me," Cody said softly. "Maybe tomorrow."

"You always say, 'maybe tomorrow.' When is tomorrow gonna come? I've been flying for a couple of weeks now and you won't fly with me. Are you scared?" Buggy asked with a slight smile.

"N-n-no, I'm not scared of flying!" Cody replied sharply. "I just don't like flying at night. That's all."

"Well, you don't fly in the daytime do ya?" Buggy asked while slowly swinging from the beam.

"I think you should leave now," Cody demanded while pointing her wing in the direction of the vent. "My parents will be home soon. Maybe . . ."

"I know!" Buggy interrupted. "Maybe tomorrow."

Buggy slipped back through the vent and flew past the window. Angered by what Buggy had said, Cody found herself talking out loud.

"I'm not scared to fly! I just, well perhaps I, maybe I, . . . I just can't see too well," Cody said sadly. "The last time that I tried to fly,

I couldn't see anything. First, I hit a chair, then I fell into a box, and when I flew out of the box, I smashed into the window. How am I supposed to fly without hitting things?!" she shouted.

Just then, Cody stopped swinging and exclaimed, "I'll show Buggy that I'm not scared!"

Cody dropped down from the ceiling and landed on top of a dusty old storage box. "That wasn't too bad!" Cody said cheerfully. "I'll try flying from here to that tall thing across the room. Here goes nothing." Cody stepped back, ran forward, flapped her wings, and took off. "I'm flying. Hey! . . ." Just as Cody got airborne she slammed into a mirror and slid down to the floor. There she sat rubbing her head with her wing. "That hurt," she said turning to look into the mirror. "I can't believe it. I flew into a mirror. I tried to fly to something that was a reflection in a mirror," she said while laughing and rubbing her head. "My eyesight is worse than I thought. I can't really make out objects until I am right near them, and that's when it's too late."

Cody paused because she heard a faint noise from above. "Mom? Dad? Is that you?" she asked. "Did you catch anything good to eat?" There was no reply, but the faint noise continued.

While looking in the mirror Cody located the source of the noise. She saw a blurry outline of a figure moving just above the window. As she strained her eyes to sharpen the image she moved closer. She climbed up to the beam near the window and realized that Buggy had been watching from outside. The noise that she heard was Buggy trying to conceal his laughter. Buggy entered through the vent and tried to regain his composure. "Now I know why you don't fly," Buggy said, still laughing hysterically. "You can't see and you probably couldn't fly if you had glasses."

"OK, so I can't see that well–big deal!" Cody said sharply.

"Hey, it's OK." Buggy replied. "I used to have the same problem. I still have bumps on my head from things that I flew into. But one day, I was screaming while falling to the ground and I heard something very strange," Buggy said calmly.

"What was it, Buggy?" Cody asked reluctantly. "What did you hear?"

"I heard a voice!" Buggy replied.

"A voice, huh?" Cody said, now laughing at Buggy. "I think you should talk to someone about those voices, Buggy!"

"No, Cody, that's not what I mean," Buggy replied, slightly irritated. "I discovered something! While I was screaming I heard my words leave my mouth and then return. But, when they returned the words sounded different. Sometimes they would come back super fast, and there were other times when they would come back super slow."

"So, what does this have to do with me being as blind as a bat?" Cody asked harshly.

"I learned to make different sounds, like humming, while flying. The higher I hummed, the better. Once I found a sound that I liked I used it every time that I flew. The sounds would leave my mouth, go off into the darkness, and then return. One night, I remembered what my father said a long time ago. 'Son, find your sound. Let the night air carry it off into the distance. If it returns then it's a gift called an echo given to you by the god of sound. Use the gift wisely and it will always tell you what to do.' I never understood what he meant until I started flying," Buggy said peacefully. "From that day on I learned to use echoes to locate objects like houses, trees, and even food. When my echo would return quickly it meant that I was flying toward something and I needed to be careful. But when my echo took a long time to return or didn't return at all, I knew that it was safe to fly."

"OK, that sounds great, but what about my eyes?" Cody asked in a concerned voice. "I'd rather have the gift of sight!"

"Cody, that's my whole point!" Buggy replied. "You don't need to rely on your eyes as much as you think you do! Use your ears. They work better than your eyes. Trust me!"

Cody and Buggy spent the next few nights trying to find a sound that Cody could use while flying. Three days and two nights passed and finally Cody was ready. On the third night, Buggy called Cody and she cautiously slipped through the vent. Cody and Buggy stood for several minutes on the ledge just above the front stoop. "It's time," Buggy said as he flew off into the darkness. "Come on, Cody. Trust your ears!" Buggy said with every pass made.

Finally, Cody took a deep breath, closed her eyes, lifted her wings, and jumped into the night. She was falling like a rock, head first toward the ground.

"Make your sound, Cody!" Buggy yelled frantically. "Flap your wings."

All of a sudden Cody screamed, "I'm scared!" In an instant her words returned to her. Then she remembered, "My sound—make my sound and listen for the gift. Trust my ears!" In that moment she hummed just as loud and as hard as she could. She flapped her wings and flew back up into the air. She just missed the ground. Cody dodged several trees, two houses, one streetlight, and four telephone wires and flew back to the ledge just above the front stoop. There she stood, her eyes larger than saucers and her knees knocking together.

Buggy joined her. "You were great!" he said while trying to catch his breath. "It felt great, didn't it?"

"Yeah, it felt pretty good!" Cody replied, clinging to the ledge and vent with her feet and hands. "You were right," she said with her heart racing. "I didn't need to rely on just my eyes. I could see with my ears. Well, you know what I mean," Cody said with a hint of a smile.

"Yeah, I know," Buggy cheerfully replied.

"Thank you for your help, Buggy," Cody said.

"No problem, Cody," he replied. "Now will you fly around with me?"

"OK, but before we leave, you have to tell me where you got the name Buggy," Cody said, moving toward the edge of the ledge.

"Well, you know how some bats eat fruit and some eat blood? Well I eat bugs and that's how I got the name Buggy."

"I eat bugs too," Cody replied with laughter. "But no one calls me Buggy."

"Consider yourself lucky," Buggy replied, smiling.

"It's a strange name but it's kind of cute," Cody said.

"You think so?" Buggy asked happily.

"Yeah, I do," Cody said. "Now, let's fly!"

And with one big motion they flew off using their gifts to find their way through the darkness. Cody was smiling now, because she was no longer "the bat that couldn't see"!

Age: 5 and Up
Time: 10 to 20 minutes

Echo-o-o-e-e-s

Can you find your way around a room using just your voice?

Get it

Chair

Cookie sheet or flat piece of cardboard

Cardboard tube or rolled piece of paper

Kazoo or whistle (optional)

Read it

✓ *Before starting the activity, explain the following to the child:*

If you make a loud noise in a room, you may hear an echo. An echo is a sound that bounces off an object like a wall and returns to your ears. The closer you are to a wall, the faster the echo returns; the farther away you are, the slower the sound returns.

✓ *You might want to read "The Bat That Couldn't See" before doing this activity.*

✓ *A kazoo or whistle can be used in place of the humming.*

Do it

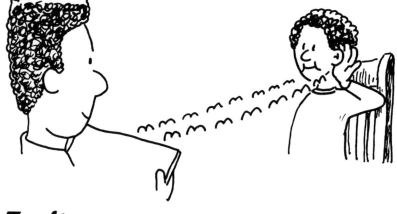

Try it

Make bat ears. Cut a couple of pieces of construction paper long enough to form a band around the child's head. Tape the strips together. Draw and cut out a pair of large bat ears and tape them to the strip of construction paper. Make sure that the bat ears are taped close to the position of the child's own ears.

Make bat masks. Look through a book about bats and draw several bat faces on construction paper. Cut out the faces, tie a string to the sides of the mask, and put it on.

Go outside and sit on the ground. With both eyes closed, try to identify the sounds you hear.

The Echo-o-o-e-e-s Challenge. Clear a path to a bare wall. Have the child stand a few feet away from the wall. Tell her to close her eyes and walk slowly toward the wall while humming. Tell her to stop just before her feet or nose touches the wall. Measure the distance from her feet or nose to the wall. Take turns walking toward the wall to see who can get the closest to the wall without hitting it.

1. Have the child sit in a chair, make a loud humming sound, and hold the sound for as long as she can. While the child is humming, slowly pass the cookie sheet or piece of cardboard in front of her face. Ask the child to tell you when she hears an echo.

2. Repeat step 1, this time standing a few feet away from the child. Ask her if she can hear an echo. When the cookie sheet is farther away, the child will have to hum louder to hear an echo.

3. Now, ask the child to close her eyes and continue humming while you walk slowly toward her holding the cookie sheet or piece of cardboard. Ask her to tell you to stop just before the cookie sheet touches her face.

4. Compare the sound of echoes made inside to echoes produced outside of your house. Talk or hum into a cardboard tube or rolled paper while you are in the following places: bathtub, fairly empty room, room with carpet, room without carpet, near the side of a building, and garage.

Think about it

Echoes are sound waves that reflect or bounce off the surface of an object and return to your ears. When sound waves hit a soft surface, a very faint echo or no echo is created. Sound waves that hit a hard surface create a loud or strong echo. When bats fly, they use echoes to find their way through the dark. While a bat is flying, it constantly sends out a high-pitched sound or click. These sounds hit an object and then return to the bat as echoes. The faster the echo returns, the closer the bat is to an object. The longer it takes for the echoes to return, the farther away an object is. The use of echoes as a means to locate or move away from objects is referred to as echolocation. Humans are not very good at echolocation. However, bats are so good at it that they can fly into the depths of the darkest cave or through a dark forest even on nights with no moon.

Age: 3 and Up
Time: 10 to 20 minutes

Betcha Can't Find It!

Can you camouflage a fish so that someone else can't find it?

Get it

Fish pattern (provided on page 41)

White paper

Scissors

Crayons or markers

Glue stick or paste

Tape

Read it

✓ *To save time, we suggest that you complete step 1 before you start the activity with the child.*

✓ *The colors used in this activity can be substituted for any colors you like.*

✓ *Be aware that tape may peel paint off of doors and walls.*

COVER

TRACE

CUT

Do it

1. Using the fish pattern provided and white paper, make three fish tracings (one for each of you and an extra) and cut them out.

2. Give the child a fish and ask him to color or deco-rate it any way he would like. Here are a few sug-gestions: stars, circles, dots, letters, numbers, or colors. You should decorate a fish too.

3. Give the child a white sheet of paper and explain that he must color or decorate the paper so it matches the colors and decorations on the fish. For example, if the fish is decorated with big and small red stars, then the paper must be covered with big and small red stars. This will become the hiding place for the fish.

Try it

- Repeat this activity, only this time use newspaper to make your fish and a background.
- Substitute construction paper for the white paper.
- Camouflage your face with face paint or make-up or make a cam-ouflage mask from a paper plate.

The Can't Find It Challenge.
On a large sheet of white paper draw an underwater picture consisting of colorful rocks and seaweed—the larg-er the paper, the better. Trace and cut out more fish. Color the fish so they blend in with the underwater picture. Ask a friend to find all of the fish.

4. Paste the fish to the background and then tape the entire picture to a door. Be creative and tape your fish upside down or at an angle. Walk about 10 feet from the picture, turn around, and try to locate each other's fishes.

BETCHA CAN'T FIND ME...

I'M SORRY, I DIDN'T EVEN RECOGNIZE YOU...

Think about it

Animals use colors and markings, like stripes and dots, for two purposes. One purpose is to communicate with other animals. For example, a skunk's stripes help it to attract mates and repel enemies. But some animals use their colors and markings to camouflage or hide themselves. Markings may be used to conceal the eyes, legs, tail, or outlines of the animal's body. This makes it difficult to detect the animal's presence. In other cases, markings and colors have evolved to match the colors and the markings of the animal's environment. If the environment is full of green leaves and brown branches then the animal's markings most likely will be green and brown. An animal is camouflaged only when its markings match the natural markings of the environment.

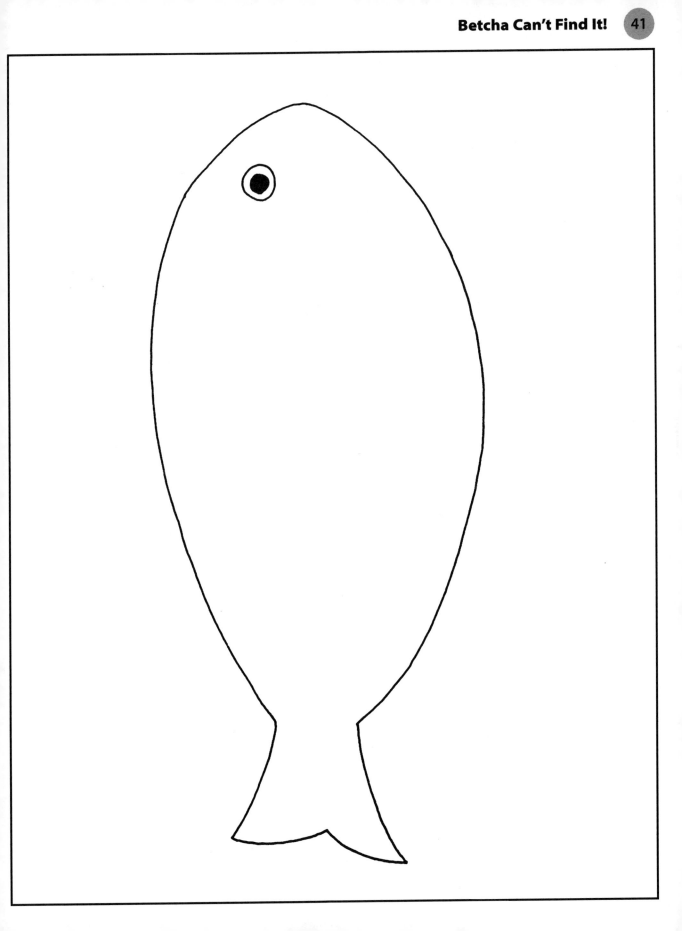

Age: 4 to 6
Time: 10 to 20 minutes

Blown Away

Can you create wind strong enough to move objects?

 ## Get it

Sheet of paper (wrapping paper, tissue paper, newspaper)

2 straws (1 fat and 1 skinny, if possible)

Fan (optional)

Hair dryer

Tape or safety pins

Table

Penny

Pencil

Book

Ball

 ## Read it

✓ Cut the paper into 10 strips, all the same length, before starting the activity.

✓ Do not allow the child to plug or unplug any electrical appliances.

✓ Make sure that you assist the child while playing with any electrical item.

✓ Never leave the child unattended.

✓ Hair dryers can overheat easily, so use the cool setting.

Do it

1. Ask the child to sit on the floor. Wave a sheet of paper in front of her face. Ask if she felt any wind. Use the straws, fan, and hair dryer to create wind. Did she feel any wind this time? Which item made the strongest wind?

2. Ask the child to wave her hands up and down in the air. Did she feel any wind? Ask her to blow on her hand using her mouth and then a straw. Which item made a stronger wind?

3. Tape or pin one end of the strips of paper to the child's sleeves and pant legs. Then walk, jump, and run around. What happened to the strips? Which movement produced the strongest wind? Try it outside. Did you notice a difference?

Try it

Investigate whether or not wind is cold or if it makes you feel cold. Use air from a fan, your mouth, and an air conditioner. Let the air blow across dry, wet, and oily skin. Which feels the coldest?

Do the "Weather Patterns" activity.

The Blown Away Challenge. Make a wind racer. Tape a straw to one side of a paper cup, thread a 10-foot piece of string through the straw, and tie each end of the string to two objects. Make sure the string is at the same height as the child's head. Now, let the child make her racer move using wind makers. Set up two or more pieces of string and have a race.

4. Place the following objects on a table: a penny, pencil, book, and ball. Have the child try to move each object with her wind makers (hands, hair dryer, straws). Did all of the objects move? Were any objects hard to move? Find five more items and try to move them with the wind makers.

 ## Think *about it*

When you waved your hand and ran around, the air around your hand and body moved faster. The faster you moved, the faster the air molecules moved. Air has a normal pressure. When you move, your body forces some air molecules to compress or bunch up. When the air molecules compress, the air pressure decreases. When you stop moving, all of the compressed air molecules spread apart and the air returns to its normal pressure. The fluctuation in air pressure creates wind.

Age: 5 and Up
Time: 10 to 20 minutes

Bricklayer

Can you build a hopscotch sidewalk using various brick patterns?

Get it

Sidewalk patterns (provided on page 48)
Pack of construction paper
Markers or crayons
1 coin

Read it

✓ The child will be jumping on the paper, so we recommend that the child play with bare feet.

✓ You can convert this to an outdoor activity using street chalk instead of paper.

✓ Young children will have a hard time throwing the coins onto the bricks when playing hopscotch, so allow them to walk up and place the coins on the numbers.

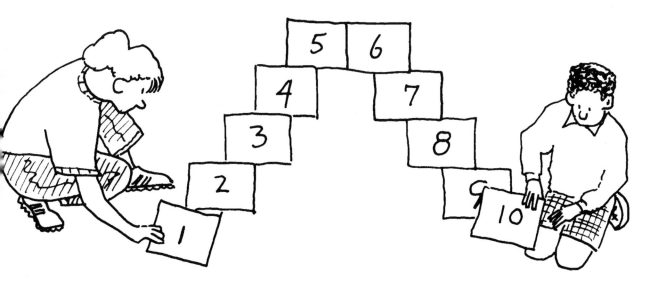

Try it

Use blank index cards and draw different brick patterns with markers. Or cut out a variety of shapes: squares, rectangles, and so on. Make five of each shape, connect your patterns together, and hold them in place with tape. This makes a great travel game.

Using a cookie cutter and cookie dough or clay, cut out 10 or more shapes. Bake the cookies and let them cool. Fit the shapes together to make an edible sidewalk pattern.

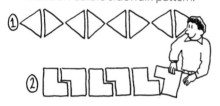

The Bricklayer Challenge. Select one of the brick patterns provided, trace it on 10 or more sheets of white paper, and cut them out. Fit the shapes together to form a short sidewalk.

Do it

1. Ask the child to choose one of the sidewalk patterns provided. Number the pieces of construction paper from 1 to 10. Use the construction paper as your bricks to build the sidewalk.

2. Play a game of hopscotch. To play, toss or place a coin on the brick marked with the number one. Jump over the brick occupied with the coin and land on the next numbered brick. Use only one foot to hop on one brick and two feet to hop on bricks that are side by side. When you get to the end, turn around and hop back down the sidewalk. Pick up the coin on your way and hop on the brick

that the coin was removed from. Then toss your coin on the next number. You lose your turn if your coin lands on the wrong number or does not land on the brick.

3. Construct the other sidewalks! What would happen if you took your favorite pattern and connected a duplicate pattern to it? What would happen if you connected a third and a fourth pattern to the first two?

I DID IT!

4. Create your own sidewalk using as many sheets of paper as you like. Have fun!

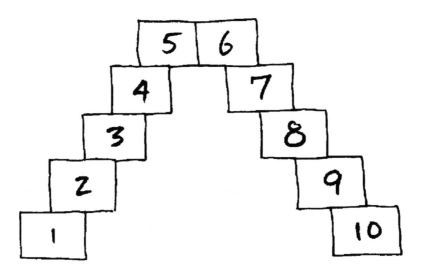

Think about it

Circles, squares, triangles, and other shapes can be found in things in nature and in things that people build, like sidewalks. Once you started to make the sidewalk pattern you continued to produce the same pattern in an orderly fashion. Any time you repeat something, you create a pattern. Patterns can be made by putting different shapes together or taking them apart. Everywhere we look in nature there are patterns—in snowflakes and rocks, in leaves and flowers, and even in buildings and homes. Mathematics is the study of many kinds of patterns, including numbers and shapes. Sometimes patterns are studied because they help to explain how the world works.

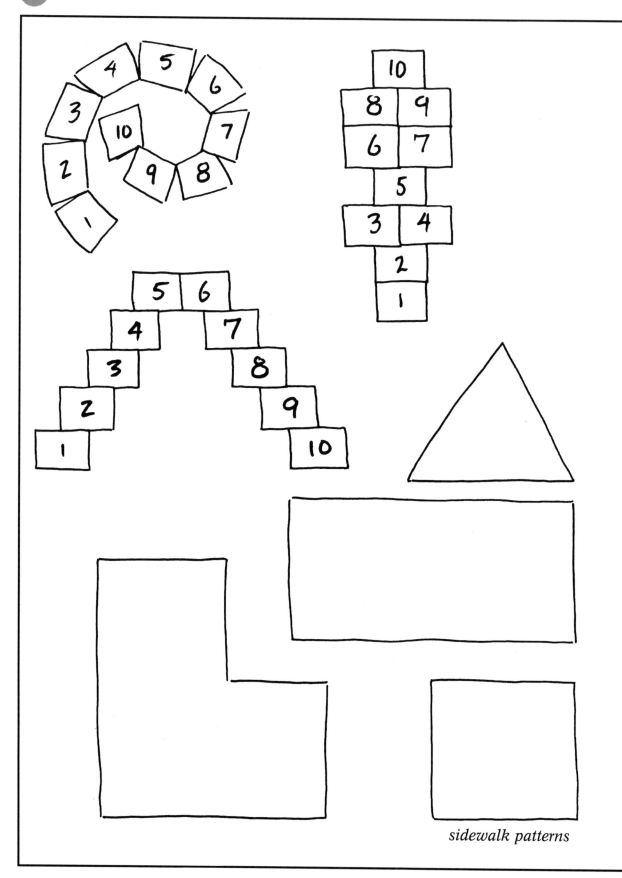

sidewalk patterns

Age: 3 and Up
Time: 10 to 20 minutes

Bubble Monster

Can you create a large monster from bubbles?

Get it

Scissors

2 trash bags

Table or counter top

Tape

¼ cup of liquid detergent
(Joy works best)

1 tablespoon of glycerin or sugar

1 cup of water

Small pan or bowl

Straws or coffee stirrers (stirrers work best)

Spatula

Strainer

Coat hanger

Read it

✓ *Make sure that the child does not swallow the bubble solution.*

✓ *Glycerin works the best and can be purchased inexpensively at a drugstore.*

✓ *Be careful using scissors to cut open the trash bags.*

✓ *When working with a young child, have him practice blowing out of the straws or coffee stirrers before dipping them in solution.*

¼ CUP
DETERGENT

1 CUP
WATER

1 tbsp
GLYCERIN
OR SUGAR

BOWL

Try it

Have a bubble race. Carry a bubble from one side of the room to the other without it popping.

Draw with bubbles by adding food coloring to your mixture. Set a piece of white paper on the bubbles until they pop. Use crayons or markers to make crazy pictures out of the bubble prints.

Blow a bubble into a friend's hands. Work together to create a giant bubble that can be held.

The Bubble Monster Challenge.

Make bouncing bubbles. You have to decide how much additional glycerin or sugar you need to make a bubble strong enough to bounce. Cut a hole in a paper plate or cup and dip it into your solution. Wave the plate from side to side and watch the bubble bounce.

Do it

1. Cut open two plastic trash bags. Cover the table or counter top with one of the trash bags and tape the corners of the bag under the table or counter to keep it from sliding. Place the other bag on the floor.

2. Help the child mix the liquid detergent, glycerin or sugar, and water in a pan or bowl.

3. You and the child each grab a handful of stirrers. Place one end of the stirrers in the solution and then blow bubbles onto the covered table. If the bubbles pop when they touch the plastic, pour a small amount of the solution onto the table, then try blowing the bubbles again.

4. Cover the entire table with bubbles. Make your monster tall and wide. Create arms for your monster that will float in the air. Place the stirrers into the solution and blow while slowly moving away from the solution.

5. Blow bubbles with the spatula, strainer, or coat hanger.

Think about it

Bubbles are made from water, and water contains molecules. Molecules are small parts of something larger. A single raindrop is made up of a lot of small molecules. When soap is added to water, the water molecules spread apart. This produces a flexible film, which can be stretched like a balloon. Glycerin or sugar joined with the soap and water and made the bubble even stronger. The glycerin and sugar also kept the bubble from quickly evaporating. When you blew on the mixture, the film stretched and pulled together around your breath forming a bubble. The colors visible in your bubbles came from light reflecting on the bubbles' surface. The thicker the bubble, the more brilliant the colors appeared. The black spots that appeared indicated that the bubble's skin was slowly evaporating and would soon pop.

Age: 5 and Up
Time: 10 to 20 minutes

Build a Better Chair

Can you build a chair with paper cups and cardboard?

Get it

- 25 or more paper cups
- 1 12-inch-square piece of cardboard

Read it

✓ The cups can be purchased in large numbers for just a couple of dollars. Having a few extra cups will allow you to do the activity more than once.

✓ Do not use cups that have been flattened or slightly bent.

✓ For safety reasons, spot the child during this activity.

![Do it]

1. Give the child one cup and have her place it upside down on the floor.
2. Ask her to stand on the cup with one foot. What happens to the cup?

3. Help her place 20 cups next to each other in four rows. Place the cardboard square on top of the cups to form a chair. Ask the child to sit on the chair. Did the cups crumble?
4. While the child is sitting on the chair, slowly remove one cup at a time. How many can you remove before the chair collapses? Count the cups underneath the cardboard. This will be the total number of cups needed to support the child's weight.

Try it

Instead of placing a cardboard square on top of the cups, use a cardboard box. Fill the box with books and toys. Try to guess how many objects will fit into the box before the cups give way.

Make supports with eggshells. Save about four shells (two eggs); trim their edges so they are all about the same size. Place the open ends of the shells on the table and cover with a book. See how many books you can stack on top of the shells.

Use your math skills. Repeat the activity and stop after step 4. Divide the child's weight by the total number of cups remaining. The answer will tell you approximately how much weight each cup can hold.

The Better Chair Challenge. Can you make the same chair using folded sheets of paper instead of paper cups? You will need several sheets of paper. The challenge is to figure out how to fold the paper so that it will be strong enough to support your weight. Feel free to use tape. Before you try to sit on the chair, we strongly suggest that you test the strength of the chair by placing books on it first.

5. Experiment with different numbers and arrangements.

6. Try to make a chair for two people or a two-tier chair.

 *Think about it*

Each time you sit in a chair the legs shorten or compress. You don't notice the compression unless a leg breaks. The same thing occurred with the chair made of cups. One cup was not strong enough to hold you up so it collapsed. When you added more cups, your weight was distributed over all of the cups. Each cup was holding a small part of your total body weight. You cannot always see or feel the cups compress. Any time your body weight is greater than the cups' ability to support your weight, the cups collapse.

Busy Bodies

Can you perform fun and unusual tasks with different parts of your body?

Get *it*

Body cards (provided on page 58)
Scissors
Paper

Read *it*

✓ *To save time, if you can, make a photocopy of the body cards provided and cut them out. If you cannot photocopy the cards, trace the cards onto a white sheet of paper.*

✓ *We recommend that you copy and cut the cards before starting this activity. However, if your child likes to cut, then let him help you cut out the cards.*

Do *it*

READ 'EM AND WEEP...

1. Copy and cut two sets of the body cards. You should have 28 cards. Shuffle the cards and deal six cards to yourself and six to the child. Once you get the hang of the game, add more cards.

2. Ask the child to place one card picture-side up on the table or floor. Ask her to give you a task to perform with the pictured body part. For example, the child will put down a "hands" card and tell you to clap. Here are a few tasks that you may use: pick up a pillow with your knees, carry a book on your head, pick up a crayon with your toes, and carry coins on your elbow. Make up your own fun tasks and add them to this list.

3. Using the same 12 cards, ask the child to name a task like jumping, running, throwing a ball, or smelling flowers. You must lay down the card(s) that would be used for that task. For example, if the child asks you to run, put down the "foot" card.

Try it

Lie on the floor with your hands folded across your chest. Without using your hands, stand up. Try it again. This time lie on your stomach with your hands to your sides.

Raise your eyebrows, cross your eyes, twist your tongue, and move your ears.

Do the "Muscle Madness" activity.

The Busy Bodies Challenge. Sit on the floor back to back with the child. Lock your arms and stand straight up. Repeat the challenge, this time picking up a ball or a pillow off of the floor.

4. Combine two cards and find tasks that match. For example, with a "hand" and a "foot" card, you could tickle the child's foot or hold the child's feet and let him walk on his hands.

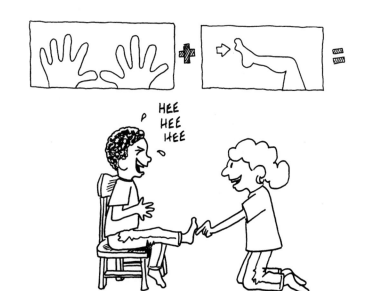

5. Try these other busy body games: pass an orange using only your chin or peel a banana or an orange using only your mouth. Try to thumb wrestle by forming the letter C with your hands and locking your fingers together. Leave your thumbs free to capture your opponent's thumb. Make up three more busy body games!

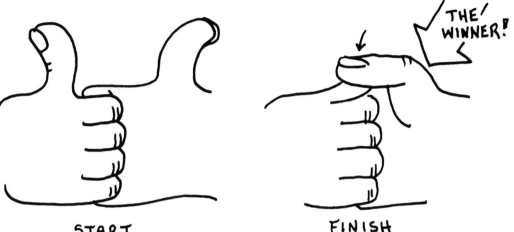

START   FINISH

Think about it

For almost every movement you make you need two things—bones and muscles. The bones in your body all join together to make up your skeleton. Your skeleton gives you your shape. Your bones are not all the same shape and size. Some bones are big, some small, some straight, and others curved. Bones are built like tubes. There is hard bone on the outside and soft bone in the middle. Bones protect and support your body. The places where the bones meet, like your knees and knuckles, are called joints. Your spine is made up of a lot of bones, which are joined like links in a chain. This allows you to make the movements called for in this activity. Your muscles cover the skeleton and are used to move it. Muscles are attached to the bones by tendons.

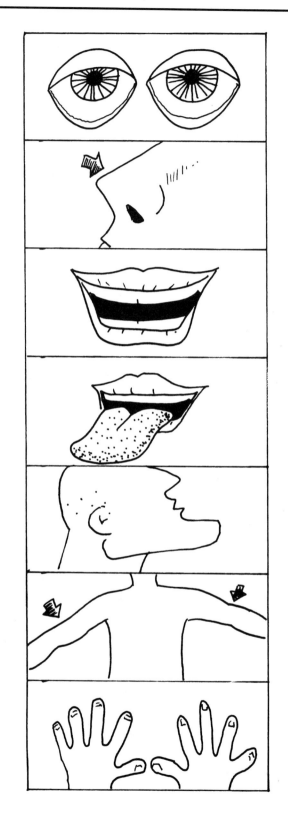
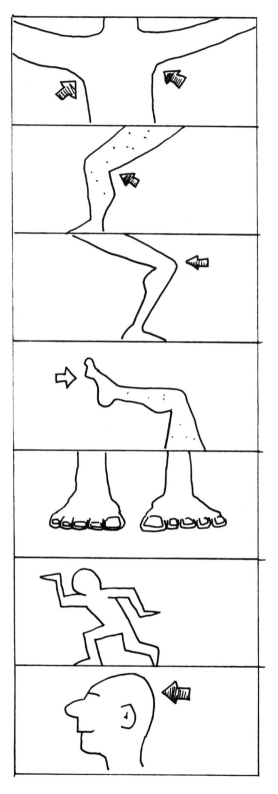

body cards

Age: 3 and Up
Time: 10 to 20 minutes

Color Dance

Can you make colors dance?

Get it

- 1 cup of milk (whole or 2 percent)
- Baking pan (foil or glass)
- Food coloring (2 or more colors)
- Liquid soap
- White paper or paper towels

Read it

✓ If you plan to do this activity more than once, you will need more than 1 cup of milk.

✓ This is a great way to use outdated milk. (Trust us. The milk mixture will not smell bad.)

✓ Cut the white paper into 4-by-4-inch squares. Do this before you start the activity.

Try it

● ● ● ● ● ● ● ● ● ● ● ● ● ●

Slowly fill a cup with water until the water forms a small dome above the rim of the glass. Ask the child to guess how many coins can be dropped into the container before the water overflows. Write down her guess while she carefully places the coins in the cup.

Cut a triangle from a piece of cardboard to make a boat. Coat the bottom of the boat with a crayon. This will temporarily prevent the cardboard from getting wet. Fill the sink with water and place the boat on the water. Add a drop of liquid soap behind the boat and watch what happens.

Do the "Dress a Salad" activity.

The Color Dance Challenge. Make colors dance in different liquids, such as water, soda, and oil. Add food coloring and soap. If you're bold, add a beaten egg yolk to each liquid mixture. Determine which liquid(s) produced the best dancing colors.

Do it

1. Ask the child to pour a cup of milk into the pan.

2. Ask her to add five or more drops of each color to the milk, putting each drop in its own area of the pan.

3. Have the child squeeze one drop of soap on top of each color. Or let the soap run down the sides of the pan. Did anything happen?

4. While the colors are moving, add more colors to the pan. See if the colors move differently when you add drops of soap from the corners or the center of the pan.

5. Help the child lightly place a sheet of paper or paper towel on top of the colors for one or two seconds. Remove the paper and let it dry.

6. If the colors stop dancing, add more milk, colors, and soap. Or rinse out and dry the pan and start again.

Think about it

Milk is made of water and butter fat, but they do not mix well at all. The two liquids do not dissolve in each other. Tiny drops of fat remained suspended in the water. This is called an emulsion. In this activity, soap is needed to stabilize the emulsion and prevent it from separating. But at the same time the soap causes the water molecules to spread apart slightly or loosen. Because water molecules are grouped so close together, they form a tight skin or have surface tension. When soap is added, the molecules spread apart or the surface tension decreases. The soap has two sides—a head and a tail. The tail repels the water and the head pulls water to itself, forming a bond with the water. The tail is attracted to the fat and sticks to it. At the same time the head, which is attracted to the water, pulls away from the fat, lifting the fat to the surface. When you added food coloring, which is made of water and dye, it mixed with the water but not the fat. So, while the water molecules were moving, the food coloring was forced to move as well. This caused the colors to dance.

Age: 5 and Up
Time: 10 to 20 minutes

Dinnertime

Can you be like a spider and use vibrations to catch food in a web?

Get it

3 index cards or sheets of paper
Pen or crayon
Paper bag
Scissors
10-foot length of string
Treats (gummy worms are a fun choice)

Read it

✓ This is a great outdoor activity.
✓ You will be making signs with the index cards or paper. You need to make at least three signs, but you can make as many as you like.

SLOW MEANS THE WIND...
FAST MEANS AN ENEMY...
MEDIUM MEANS DINNER!

1. On one card, write the word *wind*. On the second card, write the word *enemy*. On the last card, write the word *dinner*. Place all three cards in a bag and set aside until step 5.

2. Cut a 10-foot piece of string. Tie it to two solid objects like a tree and a fence post 10 feet apart. Make sure that the string is taut.

3. Ask the child to stand at one end of the string with his back to you. Ask him to lightly hold on to the string. As you stand at the other end of the string, pluck the string at fast, slow, and medium speeds. Ask him if he can feel the difference between the vibrations.

4. Read the following story to the child:

You are a hungry young spider. You have just spun your first web and you are waiting to catch your first meal. While waiting, you start thinking about what your mother said to you about catching food. "If your web vibrates slowly, it might be the wind, so don't worry. If your web vibrates quickly and strongly, it might be an enemy, so protect yourself. But, if your web vibrates faster than the wind but slower than an approaching enemy, then it's dinnertime!"

5. The child will be the spider and you will make the vibrations mentioned in the story. You may want to practice with the child before you start the game. Get the bag that you set aside in step 1. Reach into the bag and select a piece of paper at random. This will tell you the type of vibration to create.

6. If you have the "wind" card, make a soft vibration. If the spider turns to chase you, you get to be the spider because the spider is making a mistake if he chases the wind. If you have the "enemy" card, you must catch the spider before he runs away. If you are "dinner" then you must walk halfway up the string and create a medium vibration. Then turn and run back down the string. If you get back before the spider catches you, you get to be the spider. If you get caught, you have to give the spider a treat. You both must hold onto the string the entire time. If you let go, stop the game and start again.

Try it

Make a giant web across the floor. Tie several pieces of string to the legs of tables and chairs. Try to step into each space without touching the string.

Go on a vibration hunt. Search your house for objects that vibrate, like a clock, a vacuum cleaner, or a purring cat.

Do the "1-800-Cup-Talk" activity.

The Dinnertime Challenge. Catch vibrations with a balloon. Hold a balloon in front of a radio speaker and feel the vibrations.

Think about it

GOTCHA!

When the string vibrated, it communicated that something was present, causing the string to vibrate. You had to decide whether it was the wind, an enemy, or food. The string vibrated much the way a guitar string vibrates when plucked. These vibrations made the spider aware of movement, and like a real spider you were able to tell the difference between the wind vibrating the web and an insect. Spiders have very sensitive feet, which helps them "hear" what is in their web.

Age: 5 and Up
Time: 10 to 20 minutes

Dress a Salad

Can you dress a salad without using clothes?

Get *it*

Empty jar with a lid
Measuring spoons
Measuring cup
Honey
Salt
Water
Paprika
Oil
Vinegar
Ground black pepper
Salad ingredients such as lettuce and tomatoes
2 bowls
2 forks

Read *it*

✓ Take all labels off of the empty jar using warm water and soap.

✓ Cut up the salad ingredients and place them in plastic bags before starting the activity with the child.

✓ Make substitutions if the child is allergic to any of the ingredients.

✓ Look through cookbooks for other dressing recipes.

Do it

1. Place an empty jar in front of the child, and help her measure and pour the following into the jar: 1 tablespoon of honey, ½ teaspoon of salt, 2 tablespoons of water, 2 teaspoons of paprika, ¼ cup of oil, 4 tablespoons of vinegar, and a pinch of pepper.

2. Place the lid tightly on the jar. Let the child shake the jar for about 30 seconds. Place the jar on the counter. Did everything mix together?

3. Set the salad dressing aside and collect your salad items. Ask the child to choose different salad ingredients and create her own salad.

4. Look at the dressing before you pour it. Have the liquids separated? If they have, you will see two layers of liquids. Has the pepper collected in one place? What happened to the paprika?

Try it

Pour oil, water, and syrup into a tall clear glass. What happened? Try to pour the water out of the glass without pouring out the other liquid.

Pour just oil and water into a jar and drop food coloring into the liquids to create rainbow drops.

Pour slightly cooled hot chocolate into a clear glass. Add milk, and/or whipped cream, and/or marshmallows.

Do the "Color Dance" activity.

The Dress a Salad Challenge.
Make a salad dressing using sour cream or mayonnaise, tomato paste, lemon juice, and salt. Experiment to find out how much of each item you will need to make it taste the way you like.

5. Shake the jar again to mix the ingredients. Then, dress your salad and enjoy.

Think about it

Some liquids, like water and vinegar, will mix together. But not all liquids will mix together. Water and oil will mix for a short time before they separate from each other. This is because liquids and other objects, like humans, have different densities. When you poured the oil in with the water and vinegar, the oil floated on top because it is less dense than water and vinegar. The density of each liquid is determined by its molecules. The amount and the size of a liquid's molecules cause them to sink or float. When you added pepper to the water, it did not mix. The pepper just floated in the liquid because of its density.

Age: 4 to 6
Time: 10 to 20 minutes

Driver's Test

Can you follow directions well enough to pass your driver's test the first time?

Get it

Medium or large cardboard box

Green, red, and yellow construction paper

Scissors

Glue

4 paper plates

Brad—a thin wire nail with a small head (optional)

String or yarn

Read it

✓ *Find a box that still has its bottom glued together.*

✓ *Cut a large circle out of the green construction paper and another circle out of the red and yellow paper. Glue the circles to the paper plates to make them more durable. Do this before you start the activity with the child.*

Do it

1. Tuck the flaps inside the box leaving one of the small flaps out. Glue a paper plate to the small flap to make a steering wheel, or attach the plate with a brad.

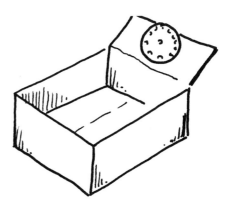

2. Place the box on the floor and ask the child to stand in it facing the steering wheel. Draw a large square around the child's feet. Cut out the square and make sure the hole provides the child with enough room to move his legs.

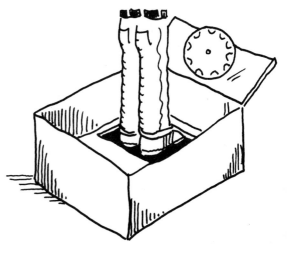

3. Using the scissors, make a small hole in both long sides of the box. Tie the string through the holes. Ask the child to stand in the box. Help him place the string around the back of his neck to hold the box up.

4. Ask the child to stand across the room or down the hall in his car. Tell him you will stand with your back to him and hold up the colored circles. Tell him to move quickly toward you when you hold up the green circle, slowly when you hold up the yellow circle, and to stop when he sees the red circle. Tell him you will turn around when you're holding up the red circle to see if he is moving. If you catch the child moving, then he has to start all over. When the child makes it all the way to you without breaking any rules, then he passes his driver's test.

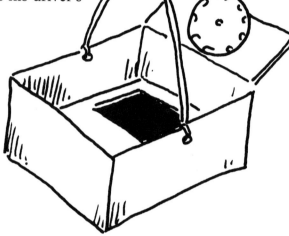

Try it
• • • • • • • • • • • • • •

Take a walk around your neighborhood. Identify the meaning of different colored signs. Do some colors have more than one meaning?

Make a driver's license for the child if he passes the test.

The Driver's Test Challenge. Try the "A-Maze-N Colors" activity.

Think about it

Your eyes saw the light that was hitting the circles and your brain told you whether the colors were green, yellow, or red. Recognizing the colors was only one part of the game. Each color had to be assigned a meaning. Once you understood what the colors meant in this activity you were able to play the game. The colors gave you information that you needed in order to play the game. Color communicates information to us every day. However, if we do not know what a certain color means, we may not respond to it appropriately.

Age: 3 and Up
Time: 10 to 20 minutes

Edible Bridge

MUNCH MUNCH

Can you build a foot-long bridge that you can eat?

Get it

12-inch ruler
6 cubes of cheese
Peanut butter
Knife
Box of square crackers
Various objects to stack on the bridge (fruit, sticks of butter, and so on)
Camera (optional)

Read it

✓ Make sure that all hands are clean when working with food.

✓ Younger children could choke on food items; watch them carefully.

✓ Cut six small blocks of cheese the same size before you begin.

✓ The camera is for the final step in the activity.

Do it

1. Place a 12-inch ruler on a table. Help the child place the cheese along the side of the ruler every two inches. Remove the ruler.

Try it

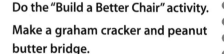

Do the "Build a Better Chair" activity.

Make a graham cracker and peanut butter bridge.

Make a floating bridge. Collect and tape closed the openings of three to five soda cans, or use plastic soda bottles. Tie them together, place them in water, and watch them float. Place a few objects on the floating bridge.

The Edible Bridge Challenge. Make a gelatin bridge. Follow the directions on a box of gelatin. Add some extra gelatin from a second box to your mixture so it will be thicker. Pour the gelatin mixture in a baking pan and let it set for at least one hour. Cut one long gelatin strip and several small squares. Support the long strip with the squares.

2. Ask the child to spread the tops of the cheese cubes with peanut butter. Help him place one cracker on top of the first and second cubes of cheese.

3. Place the second cracker next to the edge of the first cracker and on top of the second and third blocks of cheese. Let the child do this until all of the cheese blocks are covered, forming a bridge.

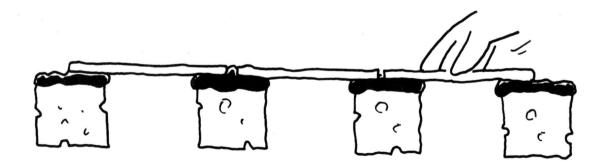

4. Test the strength of your bridge. Stack objects like sticks of butter, blocks of cheese, or fruit on your bridge. How many objects will the bridge support before it collapses?

5. Take a picture of your bridge or while you are eating.

Think about it

When you constructed your bridge, you had to make sure that it would stand up. You used the cheese squares to make supports for the bridge. The cheese helped the bridge support the weight of the objects or loads placed on it. A bridge must be strong enough to support its load. A load is something that moves over a bridge, like cars, trucks, or people. The weight of the bridge was spread across all of the cheese supported. In other words, each piece of cheese supports a small part of the bridge's total weight. To make sure that a bridge is strong, engineers choose strong materials. They also decide where the bridge needs extra supports so that it will not fall.

Age: 6 and Up
Time: 10 to 20 minutes

Eye Need a Hand

Can you draw an object that you can feel but not see?

Get it

Shoe box
Tape
10 to 12 pieces
of white paper
Scissors
Crayons
Variety of objects such as a key, eye-glasses, a candle, a toy car

Read it

✓ *Make sure you choose objects that feel different from each other, and keep them hidden from the child until you're ready to use them.*

✓ *Make sure that you provide comfort if the child is discouraged by the outcome of her drawings.*

Do it

1. Help the child cut a hole in one of the long sides of the shoe box. Make it big enough to fit the child's hand into it.

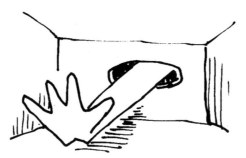

2. Using only two pieces of tape, attach a sheet of paper to the bottom of the box. You may need to cut the paper so it will fit inside.

3. Ask the child to select a crayon, place her hand inside the box, and draw a square without looking.

You may want to place the lid on the box.

4. When she has finished drawing the square, take the paper out of the box. Ask her to draw the square again, but let her look this time. Which drawing looked more like a square?

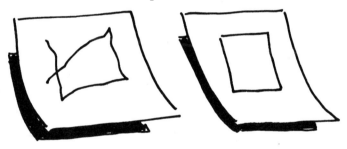

5. Place a new sheet of paper in the box and ask her to try drawing the following: the letter *X*, a circle, a face, and a house. Use a new sheet of paper after each drawing.

6. Now, remove all tape and paper from the box. Place one of the objects collected in the box without letting the child see the object.

Try it

Create mystery socks and boxes.
Place an object into a sock or box and ask the child to feel the object through the sock or tilt it around in the box. Have the child try to guess the object and draw her prediction. This is great for parties!

Draw a letter, number, or shape on someone's back with your finger.
Ask them to guess what you drew.

Do the "Fantastic Finger Feats" activity.

Try the "Peek-a-Boo Picture" activity.

The Eye Need a Hand Challenge.
Write the letter *A* in big print on a sheet of paper with a crayon. Place the tip of a second crayon anywhere on the letter. Close your eyes and have the child tell you how to trace over the letter.

7. Ask the child to place one hand in the box and feel the object. Give her a piece of paper and ask her to draw a picture of the object. Remind her that she cannot look at the object in the box. Compare the drawing to the object in the box. How does it look?

8. Repeat this for all of the objects collected. After comparing the objects to her drawings, ask the child to look at the objects and draw them. Was it easier to draw the objects when looking?

Think about it

When you draw, you use your eyes and your hands. Your brain helps to control the movement of your hands and helps you understand what you see. It becomes difficult to make your hands do what you need them to do when you can't see them. When you touched the object in the box, you had to create a mental picture of the object. The picture was created because the nerves in your hands sent information about the object to your brain. Then your brain put the information together to make a picture of the object. It is easier to guess the objects when they do not feel the same. It is also easier to guess the objects when they are familiar.

Age: 4 to 7
Time: 10 to 20 minutes

Fantastic Finger Feats

Can your fingers lift, snap, flick, catch, and spread with ease?

 ## Get it

Pencil
A small ball like a tennis ball
Cup with a handle
Coin
Table
Ruler

Read it

✓ *You can make a ball out of aluminum foil if you don't have a small ball.*

✓ *Take a break if the child's hands get tired from doing this activity.*

Do it

1. Ask the child to sit on the floor and pick up a pencil by pinching it between his fingers. Start with the thumb and first finger, then move to the first finger and second finger, and so on. Try it with the other hand. With which fingers, if any, was it most difficult to pick up the pencil?

2. Have the child carry a small ball across the room using one finger from each hand (use the right-hand thumb and left-hand first finger). Were there any problems?

3. Use one finger to lift a cup by the handle off of the floor. Ask the child to repeat this using each of his fingers. Which, if any, were the weak fingers?

4. Have the child try to snap his fingers by pressing his thumb against each finger and sliding the fingers apart in opposite directions. Try the other hand. Was there a snapping sound? Which fingers made the loudest sound?

5. Place a coin on a table. Ask the child to flick the coin across the table. Have him repeat this for each finger without using his thumb. What happened?

6. Ask the child to rest his arm on a table with his wrist hanging off of the edge. Ask him to cup his hand as if holding a glass, and then drop a ruler between his fingers. Ask the child to grab the ruler as it passes between his fingers. Repeat for the other hand. Did he grab it?

7. Ask the child to hold his hand off the edge of the table with his palm facing the floor. Drop the ruler between his fingers (thumb and first finger, first finger and second finger, and so on). Was it hard for the child to catch the ruler this way? Try this with the other hand. Which hand worked the best?

Try it

Have the child push the buttons on a calculator, computer, or telephone with his strong hand, as fast as possible. Then, try the same task as quickly as possible with his weak hand.

Repeat the activity using the toes.

Do the "Muscle Madness" and "Eye Need a Hand" activities.

The Finger Feats Challenge. Trace your hand on a sheet of white paper and cut it out. Using five flexible straws, tape one straw to the middle section of each finger cutout. Cut off any part of the straw that hangs over the top of the paper, being careful not to cut the flexible section. The flexible section of the straw resembles the joints in your fingers. Play games or pick up objects with your flexible fingers.

8. Have the child put all his fingers together and then try moving one finger at a time while keeping the other fingers together. For example, move the thumb only, then move the first finger only, and so on. Try the other hand. What happened?

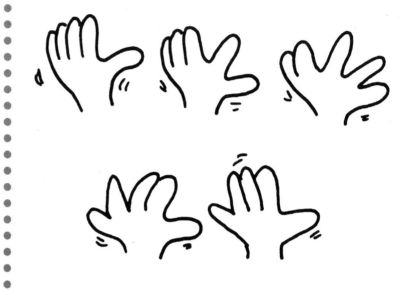

Think about it

When you picked up a pencil, flicked a coin, or spread your fingers apart they had to be flexible. Your fingers had to be able to bend, flex, stretch, and be strong enough to do this activity. The muscles in your hands allowed your bones to move so that you could complete each task. Your brain sent a message to your muscles commanding them to move your fingers. After a couple of tries your brain was able to tell your fingers how to do the task better. Learning new movements like playing a musical instrument or a sport takes time and practice. You have to learn to control your muscles to perform different tasks.

Age: 5 to 8
Time: 10 to 20 minutes

Graham Cracker Castles

Can you make a castle that will not collapse when attacked?

Get it

10 graham cracker bars (you may want extras in case the child eats one)
2 paper towels
Blunt or plastic knife
Peanut butter
12 large marshmallows
Animal crackers (optional)
Toy car or anything small that rolls

Read it

✓ This activity uses the word *bars* to refer to one large graham cracker bar that is made up of four smaller bars.
✓ Use only small dots of peanut butter to hold the walls together.
✓ The toy car will be used as a battering ram.
✓ You may want to read a story about castles before or after this activity (see Suggested Reading).

Do it

1. Place four bars on a paper towel. Put small dots of peanut butter along the short edges of each bar. Help the child press the edges of two bars together. Attach the remaining bars using peanut butter to form one complete square or castle. Set the castle aside on a paper towel until step 6.

2. Dot the edges of four more bars with peanut butter. Do not stick the bars together. Set aside on another paper towel.

3. Stack three marshmallows on top of each other using peanut butter to hold them together. Make a total of four marshmallow towers.

← PEANUT BUTTER   ✕ 3

4. Using peanut butter, stick the edge of one bar set aside in step 2 to one of the marshmallow towers. Stick another bar to the tower to form an *L*. Repeat until you have formed a second castle that has marshmallow towers at the corners.

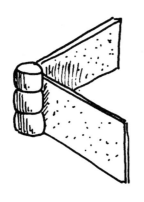

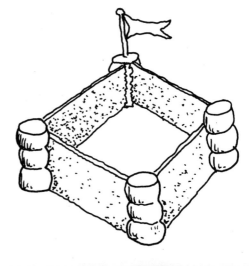

5. Help the child make bridges for the castles by coating one edge of another bar and sticking it to any side of each castle. You can support it with marshmallows. You can also populate your castle by putting some peanut butter on the bottoms of animal crackers and placing them around the castle.

6. Now, attack and smash one wall on each castle with the toy car. Did anything happen? Which castle held up during the attack?

7. Enjoy eating your castle!

Try it

Build a stronger castle using double layers of graham crackers.

Build a graham cracker house and decorate it with candies.

The Cracker Castle Challenge.
Find a book about castles and build an edible model of a real castle.

Think about it

When you attacked the walls of the two castles, you probably noticed that the castle without the towers sustained more damage. This is because the walls on the first castle were attached to each other. This meant that each wall was dependent on the other walls for support. When a wall collapsed it affected the stability of the other walls. In comparison, the marshmallows prevented the walls from collapsing on the second castle. Because the walls were not connected to each other, they did not rely on the other walls for support. Instead, the marshmallow towers offered the support that each of the walls needed. The towers prevented other walls from collapsing by absorbing some of the force produced by the toy hitting the sides of the castle.

Age: 5 and Up
Time: 10 to 20 minutes

The Great Shoe Detective

Can you tell how someone walks by looking at their shoes?

Get it

Five or more pairs of shoes

Read it

✓ Gather more than five pairs of shoes if you can. The more shoes you get the better!

Do it

1. Ask the child to help you spread the shoes out on the floor, put on a pair of someone else's shoes, and go for a short walk in the shoes. How do the shoes feel? Have the child try on the rest of the shoes. How did they feel?

2. Look at the bottom of each shoe, especially the heel. Which part of the heel is worn down? Is the sole of the shoe worn out too? Can the child determine whether the shoe's owner walks on the inside, outside, heel, or toe of the foot?

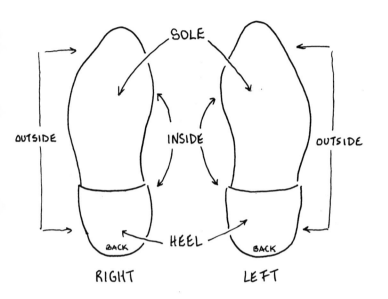

HEY! MY FEET TURN IN LIKE A BIRD!

Try it

Mix the shoes up in a pile or hide them, and then try to find their mate. Can you tell who the shoes belong to?

Place the shoes in a pile. Select a shoe condition such as a worn-down heel or worn-out sole. Have the child search for a pair of shoes that match the condition.

Place all of the shoes in a pile; make sure that your own shoes are mixed up in the pile too. Stand back about 10 feet, say "go," and run up to the pile. Select any pair of shoes, put them on, and run back to the starting line. Who won? How did the shoes feel?

Walk with your left leg and left arm moving at the same time. Hug yourself while walking; walk pigeon-toed; walk on your tiptoes and then on your heels. How did it feel?

The Shoe Detective Challenge. Try to find differences between how runners and walkers move. Go outside and watch the feet and legs of runners and walkers. Do you see any differences? Which one seems to float on air, move on her toes, or move with her feet pointing inward or outward?

3. Find your own shoes in the pile and then switch shoes with each other. Make a prediction about how the other person will walk just by looking at their shoes. Test the predictions by putting on your own shoes and watching each other walk. Was your prediction correct? Try to predict how your friends and family will walk.

Think about it

When you walk, your step begins at the heel of your foot and rolls forward to your toes. When you looked at the soles of the shoes, you could see which areas of the soles were most worn. This information told you whether the owner of the shoe walks more on the toes or heel or if the person walks from the outside of the foot to the inside or from the inside to the outside. Each person has a slightly different way of walking.

Age: 4 to 7
Time: 10 to 20 minutes

Hard Headed

Can you make a helmet strong enough to protect a ball of clay?

Get it

Lightweight ball like a tennis ball

2 pillows

Clay

5 soft items (try paper towels, a pair of socks, an old shirt, a newspaper, and cotton balls)

Small box with a lid

Read it

✓ Be careful not to drop any heavy objects on the child's head.

✓ Make sure that you pay close attention to the child during this activity. She may want to throw the balls of clay.

Do it

1. Ask the child to sit on the floor. Stand over her and gently drop a ball on her head. Ask her if she felt anything. Did the ball hurt? Now, place a pillow on her head and gently drop the ball on the pillow. Did she feel a difference? Will two pillows work better?

2. Ask the child to touch her head and tell you what she feels. Explain that her skull surrounds her brain and protects it. Ask her what might happen to her brain if she didn't have a skull.

KNOCK KNOCK

3. Ask the child to form a ball out of the clay and drop or throw the ball of clay on the floor. What happened?

4. Ask the child to reshape the clay into a new ball and wrap it in a soft item such as a newspaper or a pair of socks. Ask her to drop the ball. What happened? Do you need more protection for the ball of clay?

Try it

Go on a hunt to find objects that **have protective coverings.** A couple of ideas are: an orange and an egg. Find 10 more objects.

Drop the clay ball from two, four, and six feet. Is there a change in the shape of the clay ball at each height?

The Hard Headed Challenge. Make a protective covering for an egg. You will need at least two eggs and the protective materials listed earlier. Protect the egg and drop it from different heights without breaking the egg.

5. Have the child place the clay ball in the box and drop it. Did it lose its shape? Place the soft items (paper, an old pair of socks, and so on) in the box and place the clay ball on top. Put the lid on the box and drop it. What happened to the clay? Stand on a chair and drop the box. Did anything happen to the clay?

Think about it

When you dropped the unprotected ball of clay, it changed shape because it didn't have any protection. The box and the soft items inside protected the ball of clay by absorbing the impact of the box hitting the floor. This prevented the ball of clay from hitting the floor with a lot of speed. In a similar way, your head is designed to protect your brain from being damaged. Your brain is surrounded by a liquid cushion and hard shell. When you hit your head, the skull and liquid cushion the impact and help to keep your brain from being crushed like the unprotected clay.

Age: 4 and Up
Time: 10 to 20 minutes

Help, We Need a Bridge!

Can you build a bridge to rescue a family?

Get it

2 bath towels
White paper
Crayons or markers
Dolls
Empty boxes or cans (spaghetti, gelatin, cereal, videotape, or crayon boxes, or soup cans)
Toys
Blocks

Read it

✓ Do not place any breakable or extremely heavy objects, like glass, on any of the bridges.

✓ Do not let children climb on the bridge constructed outside without plenty of supervision.

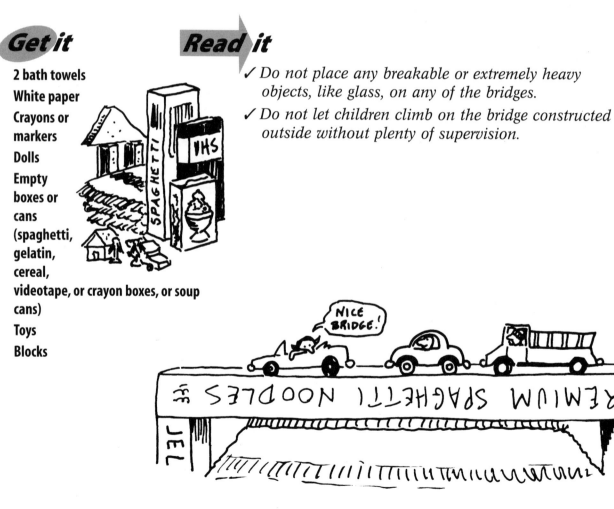

Do it

1. Read this short story to the child:

   You and your family went for a long walk through the woods to collect cherries. You crossed a wooden bridge that was over a fast-moving river and continued walking until you reached an orchard of cherry trees. After everyone had filled their pockets with cherries, you headed for home. But when you reached the riverbank you found that the bridge was gone! Now, the only way for your family to get back home is to build a new bridge!

2. Place one bath towel on the floor; it will be the river. On one side of the river have the child draw a house on a sheet of white paper. Collect toy people or dolls and place them on the other side of the river.

3. Using your boxes and blocks, help the child construct a bridge. Start by placing a spaghetti box across the top of two gelatin boxes to form a bridge. Remember that the bridge must reach across the river.

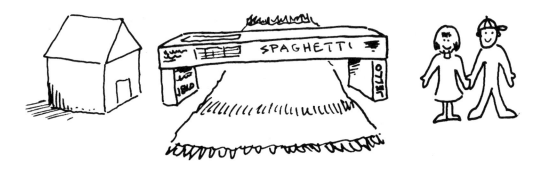

Try it

- Do the "Edible Bridge" activity.

- Make bridges outside using wood, cardboard boxes, building blocks, string, or rope.

- **Make a shoe box bridge.** Collect five or more shoe boxes, arrange them in a straight line, tape a piece of cardboard across the tops of the boxes to make a platform, and walk across your bridge.

- **The Bridge Challenge.**
  Make the towel "river" wider than the widest building material you have. Can you make a bridge that will span this very wide river?

4. When the bridge is completed, ask the child to place as many toys (cars, trucks, and so on) as possible on the bridge. How many toys can the bridge hold? You may want to record the number of toys each bridge can support.

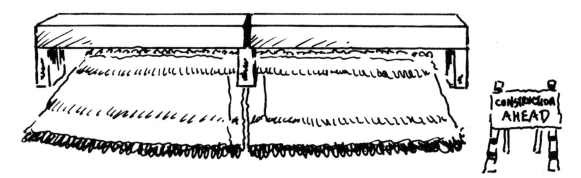

5. Continue to widen the river by placing the second towel beside the first. Help the child make new bridges that will successfully stretch across the wider river.

Think about it

When you constructed your bridge, you were working with Sir Isaac Newton's Third Law of Motion. This law says, "To every action there is always an opposed and equal reaction." When you placed a span, like the spaghetti box, across the gelatin box supports, the span pushed down on the supports. This downward push was the action. The reaction was the upward push of the supports against the bottom of the span. When you added toys or a load to the bridge, you increased the downward push, which increased the upward push of the supports. When the load on the bridge becomes too great, the supports collapse and the bridge falls down.

Age: 5 to 7
Time: 10 to 20 minutes

Keep Your Balance

Can you keep your balance using only your ears?

Get it

Book

Broom

6 empty nonbreakable containers such as soup cans, plastic soda bottles, and milk cartons

Piece of cardboard big enough to hold all six containers and to be used as a tray

Read it

✓ *This activity asks the child to play with his eyes closed, so be prepared to offer assistance.*

✓ *In step 1, be careful not to push the child too hard!*

Try it

Create a "Keep Your Balance" travel version. Pack some small objects that stand upright (juice box, paper cup, doll, or action figure) and a small cardboard square. Try to balance the objects while riding in a car.

Make a hanging mobile. Use a coat hanger, string, tape, and a lot of small objects (keys, earrings, pencils). Arrange the objects so they balance.

Do the "Total Dizziness" activity.

The Keep Your Balance Challenge.
Have a tug of war while standing on books or small boxes. Try to pull the other person off balance. Repeat while standing on one leg, with eyes closed, or with feet apart.

Do it

1. Ask the child to stand with his feet apart and give him a little push. Ask him to put his feet together and give him a push. Try again. This time ask the child to close his eyes while you push. Did he notice anything different? Repeat the positions but ask him to bend his knees. Did anything different happen?

2. Ask the child to stand on one leg with his hands on his hips and his eyes open. Try it with his eyes closed. Was there a difference? Ask him to stand on one leg with his arms outstretched and his eyes open and then closed. Notice anything different? Tell him to bend his leg. Did this change anything?

3. Ask the child to raise his arms out to the side and walk a straight line with his eyes opened, then try it with his eyes closed. Do it again, only this time ask him to walk with a book on his head. Did anything happen?

4. Help the child find the point where a broom will balance on his foot. Then, ask him to stand on one leg, raise the other leg, and balance a broom on that foot. Try it again with his eyes closed.

5. Place the containers on a table and give the piece of cardboard to the child. Ask him to put the cardboard in the palm of his hand, walk up to the table, place one object on the cardboard, and walk to the kitchen keeping the containers steady. Can he carry more than one container at a time? How many containers can he carry at one time? How fast can he walk carrying the containers?

6. Place three containers on the tray and ask the child to stand on one leg with his eyes closed. How long can he keep the objects balanced? Take turns trying this. Who can keep their balance the longest?

Think about it

Your center of gravity is the point on your body where gravity pulls on your body equally. Its position depends on the shape of your body and more important, your age. For example, children up to the age of about 12 have similar centers of gravity. However, as children mature and develop more mass, their center of gravity shifts. A grown woman's center of gravity is located near the waist due to muscle mass in her hips. A grown man's center of gravity is located near his chest due to the muscle mass in his chest and shoulders. When you walk, your weight shifts from side to side, making you unbalanced. Bending your knees moves your weight downward and helps you to balance yourself better. When you were moving with the tray your eyes and ears helped you. They told you whether you were balanced. Your eyes told your brain which way you were moving. This is why balancing is harder when your eyes are closed. The fluid in your ears also told your brain that you were moving. Your brain processed all of this information and told you how to keep your balance.

Age: 5 and Up
Time: 10 to 20 minutes

Muscle Madness

Can you move your body without using your muscles?

Get it

Chair
Radio (optional)

Read it

✓ You may need to help the child understand that her muscles allow her to move.

✓ You may have to show her where her biceps, calf, and thigh are located.

✓ If possible, have the child wear shorts and a T-shirt to allow her to feel her muscles more easily.

Do it

1. Ask the child to place her left hand on her right biceps (the upper part of her arm) and bend her right arm up and down. Ask her if she felt anything.

2. Ask the child to place her hand lightly around her throat and swallow. Did she feel anything?

3. Ask the child to sit in a chair, place one hand on her left calf (the back of her leg below her knee), and flex and point her foot repeatedly. Ask her to place one hand on her thigh (above the knee) and repeatedly bend and straighten her leg. Did she feel anything?

GULP

Try it

Wiggle your fingers and feel along your forearm with your other hand. Look at the back of your hands as you wiggle your fingers.

Make different faces and feel the muscles in your face.

Do the "Busy Bodies" activity.

The Muscle Madness Challenge.

Teach your muscles not to tire so quickly! Time how long you can hold one leg up. Practice for a few days, keep a record, and watch for improvement.

4. Ask the child to lie on her back with her hands on her stomach while pushing her stomach up and down or doing a slow sit-up.

5. Have the child place her hand on one foot and spread her toes.

6. Now, play a game of Simon Says. Use some of these movements in your game: raise both eyebrows, open your mouth, open and close both eyes, raise a finger, smile, move your nose or ears (if you can). Add more movements. Go crazy and have fun! Play the game to music.

7. Find five other things that you can do with your muscles such as dancing, throwing, and running.

Think about it

In order to do this activity your muscles had to help your bones move. Your skeleton is not capable of moving on its own. Your bones needed muscle power in order to move. Every time that you wanted to make a movement, your brain had to send a message to your muscles. When you bent your arm, you used a muscle to pull one bone toward the other. Then you used another muscle to pull the bone down again. But your muscles cannot do any work without oxygen and food. The harder your muscles work the more fuel they need. When you danced and ran around, your breathing increased. That was your muscles' way of demanding extra oxygen. As you breathed, oxygen was taken from the air and carried to your muscles by your blood. Your blood also carried food stored by your body. To get these supplies to your muscles your heart had to beat faster in order to pump the blood quickly.

Age: 3 to 6
Time: 10 to 20 minutes

The Nosy Detective

Can you use your sense of smell to find a missing scent?

Get it

10 squares of paper
Tape
5 plastic soda bottles
Pencil or pen
4 different types of fruit
Water

Read it

✓ Ask family and friends to save bottles for you.

✓ Be very careful when smelling an unknown substance. Hold the bottle near your chin and slowly squeeze. While squeezing the bottle, use the other hand as a fan to direct any odors toward your nose.

✓ You will need to do the three steps listed below before you start this activity with the child:

1. Using five squares of paper and tape, make a label for each bottle. Write one fruit name on each bottle's label. Give two bottles the same fruit label.

2. *Cut one slice from each fruit. In a cup, mash one fruit slice with a teaspoon of water. Repeat this for each fruit. Pour some of each mixture into the appropriate bottles.*

Try it

Do the activity again, but first go on a hunt for 10 different cooking scents (spices, vegetables, coffees).

Make new fruit odors. Blend two or more fruits in a blender. Ask the child to smell the mixture and identify each fruit. For example, mix a banana with a strawberry to create a "straw-banana-berry" odor.

The Nosy Detective Challenge. Collect one or more bottles of perfume. Ask the child to stand about six feet away with her eyes closed. Pour a drop of the perfume into a dish. Count how long it takes the child to smell the odor.

3. *Cover the names on all five bottles by taping the remaining squares of paper to the bottles. Write a number on each piece of paper (1, 2, 3, and 4). Mark an X on the last bottle (with the duplicate fruit).*

1. Read the following to the child: One of your favorite fruits has lost its scent. You can help find the scent by using your nose. Smell bottle *X*. Now, match that smell to one of the other bottles.

2. Place the bottles on a table in a line. Ask the child to smell bottle X first, then smell bottles one through four one at a time. After smelling each bottle she should smell the X bottle again to compare the scents.

3. Ask the child to tell you when she has found a match for the X bottle. Lift the number and read the name to find out what fruit lost its scent. Did the child find the missing scent?

Think about it

The fruits were turned into liquids by being mashed and mixed with water. When water is exposed to air, it begins to change into an invisible gas or vapor. The change from a liquid to a gas or vapor is called vaporization or evaporation. When the liquids evaporated, they were released into the air and carried to your nose. In the skin that forms the inner lining of your nose are special nerve cells that help to produce your sense of smell. These nerve cells sent a signal to your brain. Your brain interpreted the signal and sent a message to another part of the brain, which told you if the odors smelled pleasant or unpleasant, strong or weak, familiar or unfamiliar.

1-800-Cup-Talk

Can you talk to a friend using paper cups tied to more than just string?

Get it

2 paper cups or soup cans
Tape
Scissors or hammer and nail
Two 5-foot pieces of string
20 paper clips
Aluminum foil
Sheet of paper
Rubber band
Trash bag
Straw
Metal or plastic slinky (optional)
Chair

Read it

✓ *If you use cans, you will need to hammer a hole, using a nail, in the bottom of both cans in advance.*
✓ *Tape the lip of the can to prevent injuries.*
✓ *Speak clearly and softly into the cups.*
✓ *Use longer pieces of string if available.*

Do it

1. Make a small hole in the bottom of each cup. Thread one end of a piece of string through the hole in the bottom of one cup. Tie the end of the 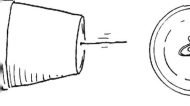 string to a paper clip inside the cup. Repeat this step using the second cup, second string, and another paper clip.

2. Link the remaining paper clips together to form a chain. Attach the ends of the chain to the free ends of each piece of string. Pull the line taut and place your hands around the mouth of the cups. Ask the child to listen while you talk into the cup, and then let the child talk. Can you hear each other clearly?

3. Remove the chain of paper clips from the string. Tear off a one-foot piece of aluminum foil, fold it in half lengthwise three times, and punch a hole in both ends. Tie the string ends through the holes and pull the string taut. Take turns talking into the cups. Can you hear better through the aluminum foil or through the paper clips?

4. Remove the aluminum foil and replace it with a

sheet of paper folded in half lengthwise three times. Take turns talking. Does the paper work better than the aluminum foil?

5. Remove the paper and attach the free ends of the

string to the following items one at a time: rubber band, trash bag, straw, and slinky (optional). Did the sound travel through these objects? Which one(s) worked the best?

Try it

Make a three-way phone. Use three pieces of string and three cups.

Make a long distance call. Try talking using 25-foot, 50-foot, and 100-foot pieces of string.

Do the "Dinner Time" and "Sounds Funny" activities, which also talk about vibrations.

The Cup Talk Challenge.

Make a cordless phone using two umbrellas and two paper cups with the bottoms cut out. Stand back to back holding the open umbrellas in front of you. Aim the cup at the center of the umbrella and speak softly while the other person listens.

6. Tie the free ends of the string to a chair and pull the string taut. If you don't hear anything, tie the strings to different parts of the chair. Does the sound travel through the chair?

7. If you can find a third person to work with, try talking to each other through his body! Tie the strings around a friend's wrists. Ask him to hold his arms out to the side while you and another person talk into your cups. Will sound travel through your friend to the other cup?

8. Find three more items that sound will travel through when you attach your cups to them.

Think about it

You make sounds when you talk. Sound is produced by molecules that vibrate or move back and forth. Sound needs something to travel through or something to carry it along. This is called a medium. Air, water, and solids like metals are all mediums that carry sound. When you spoke into the cup, the air molecules inside the cup started vibrating. These vibrations were carried along the string and into the other cup. When you connected the string to the paper clips, foil, paper, and chair, the vibrations were carried through each of the mediums. Vibrations move faster through water and some solid things like metal, than through air. Water and certain metals are made up of molecules that are more densely packed than air molecules. This means that denser material will let sound move faster. When the vibrations have a hard time moving through the object, the sound will not be as loud. When the vibrations are stopped, no sound will be heard.

Age: 3 to 5
Time: 10 to 20 minutes

Parade of Patterns

Can you make fun patterns with food?

Get it

Paper
Crayons
Knife
Bread
Peanut
butter
Jelly
Fruits
(raisins,
bananas,
and so on)

Read it

✓ Hands should be washed before doing this activity.

✓ Knives should be plastic or have blunt ends.

✓ Make sure that the child is not allergic to any of
the food items.

Do it

1. Using a sheet of paper and a crayon, draw these basic shapes: circle, square, and triangle.

Try it

● ● ● ● ● ● ● ● ● ● ● ● ● ● ● ●

Make pudding or gelatin patterns by layering two or more different types of pudding or gelatin. Use fruit or graham crackers to separate each layer.

Make patterns on a stick. Cut up a variety of fruits, such as strawberries and bananas, and slide them on a wooden skewer or toothpick and serve.

Do the "Spot the Pattern" activity.

The Parade of Patterns Challenge.
Go outside and collect 10 leaves, rocks, and sticks of various sizes, colors, and shapes. Create a parade of patterns by arranging the leaves in circles, squares, or any pattern you like. How many new patterns can you create?

2. Cut three slices of bread in half. Spread each half with peanut butter. Help the child copy the basic shapes on the pieces of bread using jelly, fruit, or other foods.

3. Place the slices of bread with shapes in a single line forming patterns or shapes. Rearrange the slices of bread to create five new patterns or make more shapes to make a longer parade.

4. Eat and enjoy your parade of patterns!

Think about it

When you arranged the slices of bread in a line, you formed patterns. Any time that you repeated shapes or orders you created a pattern. We are able to recognize patterns in foods, on buildings, and even cars, because we have pictures of these objects stored in our memory. Our brain stores information about shapes, letters, and numbers. Any time that we see numbers arranged in a specific pattern, we can recognize the meaning it has to us, such as telephone numbers, zip codes, or birthdays. Human brains are very good at recognizing patterns. In fact, the brain is better than any computer ever designed.

Age: 3 to 5
Time: 10 to 20 minutes

Peek-a-Boo Picture

Can you guess what a picture is without seeing the whole thing?

Get it

Sheet of paper thick enough that you can't see through it, such as newspaper, construction paper, or brown paper bag

Scissors

Picture book, coloring book, or illustrated magazine

Clipboard (optional)

Read it

✓ Old magazines work well for this activity.

✓ If the child is answering easily then challenge him by using a book or magazine he is unfamiliar with.

✓ Using a clipboard can make it easier to hold the pictures and the strips of paper.

✓ Do steps 1 through 3 without the child.

Do it

1. Cut a sheet of paper lengthwise into four or more strips leaving a half an inch at the end so the strips remain connected. Make sure the strips are long enough to cover a book or magazine.

2. Select a picture from the child's favorite picture or coloring book—the bigger the picture the better.
3. Place the strips of paper over the picture. Be sure to cover the entire picture.

Try it

Cover the television screen with strips of paper and randomly pause one of the child's favorite videos. Remove the strips one at a time and ask the child to identify the picture. Most video players allow you to pause for up to five minutes.

Go on a "Peek-a-Boo" objects hunt. Look around your home and neighborhood for objects that partially block the view of another object, like a tree that partially blocks the view of a house. This makes a great travel game.

The Peek-a-Boo Challenge. Cut a square in the side of a box and tape paper strips side by side covering the square. Place one of the child's toys in the box. Remove the strips one at time until the child identifies the toy.

4. Ask the child to remove one strip at a time. Ask him to identify the picture before it is completely uncovered.

5. Repeat with other pictures. Make it more challenging if necessary.

Think about it

Placing the strips of paper over the pictures obscured the view of the picture. As you removed the strips, the picture was only partially obscured. When you saw part of the picture, your brain tried to match the information to a picture that you had seen before. When your brain had enough information, you were able to recognize the object. Your ability to recognize some partially covered object is based entirely on your knowledge of that object. The more familiar you are with an object and how it works, the easier it is to identify it from limited information.

Shelly's Space Adventure

Can you imagine yourself in space?

When the 3:00 dismissal bell rang at Shepard Elementary School, Shelly Anderson was eager to leave. Shelly ran the four blocks to the apartment where she and her mother lived. She bolted up three flights of stairs, dashed down a long corridor, and stopped in front of a large gray metal door with the number 312 painted in black. She opened the door with a key attached to a pink neon shoe string that hung around her neck. As always she placed her books on the couch and called her mother: "Ms. Anderson please? Hi mom, I'm home." It was the usual conversation. Shelly was to thaw something for dinner, complete her homework, and not invite anyone over.

Shelly always did as she was told. And because she loved school she was always eager to complete her homework, but not today. Shelly could not stop thinking about how she and her fourth-grade class made history. Shelly and her classmates spoke to astronauts that were in space. She recalled how her classroom was full of TV news cameras, a large-screen TV, and a microphone with a speaker that the students used to talk to the astronauts. "Shuttle crew, this is Mission Control, do you read me? Out," Mission Control asked.

"Roger, Mission Control. We read you loud and clear. Go ahead. Out," the shuttle commander said.

"Shuttle crew, we have 23 students in Ms. Boxley's fourth-grade science class who are ready to ask you a few questions. Is that a go? Out," Mission Control asked.

"Roger, Mission Control. It's a go. Out," the shuttle commander responded.

The students lined up and one by one they began asking their questions. "What does space food taste like? How do you sleep?

111

And what do you do when you get bored?" One classmate asked, "What does it feel like to float around in space? Out."

"It feels like swimming underwater," the pilot said. "You can float in water as well as in space. So we practice working in space by working in a large water tank or pool. Out."

Another classmate asked, "What is the name of your mission? Out."

The commander of the shuttle responded, "Our mission is called 'Operation Space Station Liberty.' It is our job to build the first part of a station where people can live and work. Out."

Finally, it was Shelly's chance to ask her question. She gripped the microphone in her left hand and a piece of paper in her right hand. She took a deep breath and read the paper. "Hi, my name is Shelly and my question is 'what will keep the space station from floating off into space?' Out." Shelly placed the microphone on the table and looked at the large-screen TV while she waited for a reply.

Several seconds passed and then the mission specialist responded. "Hi, Shelly," the astronaut replied with laughter in her voice. "That's a real good question. The easiest way to answer is to say we will use the Earth's gravitational pull to keep us from drifting off into space. Gravity is the force that holds houses, people, cars, and everything else to the Earth. As you move away from the Earth the gravitational pull is not as strong. But it is strong enough to keep us in orbit."

Just then Shelly stopped daydreaming about the day she had had. "What are space stations made out of?" Shelly said out loud. "No one asked that question. What can I use to make one?" Determined to build a space station, Shelly looked around the apartment for building supplies. She collected several large storage boxes, an old bed sheet, several sheets of paper, and markers. Shelly stacked the boxes two high and placed them in a half circle. She made sure that the boxes were steady and would not fall. She remembered that one of the astronauts said, "The space station has to be balanced or it will not be safe. It could spin in a circle like a merry-go-round, float off into space, or fall out of orbit and back to Earth." Shelly took extra time to make sure that the boxes were balanced. She drew different pictures and taped them to the sides of the boxes. She drew planets, stars, comets, spaceships, and kids playing games in colorful space suits. Shelly even cut small windows in a couple of boxes. She finished by throwing a sheet over the boxes.

Shelly was pleased with her space station. However, she knew that she was not finished. "I need food, clothes, and something to play with," Shelly said. "One of the astronauts squeezed her food out of bags and wore a jumpsuit to bed." Shelly put on her red jumpsuit, stuffed some pudding in a sandwich bag, grabbed a few stuffed animals, and sat inside of her space station eating and doing her homework. Shelly's assignment was to interview a friend who lives in a space station. Just then the phone rang. "Hello," Shelly said.

DeAnna, Shelly's classmate asked, "What are you doing?"

"What do you mean?" Shelly replied in a confused voice.

"What are you doing with the boxes, and why are you running around the room like a little kid?" DeAnna asked.

"Are you lookin' in my window again?" Shelly asked, crawling out of her space station to look out of the window. "Why are you always lookin' in my window?"

"Nothin' better to do I guess," DeAnna responded quietly. "And it's better than watchin' my little brother."

"Did you write your letter?" Shelly asked.

"Naw!" DeAnna responded sharply. "And what's that gotta do with those boxes in your room?"

"It's a space station," Shelly replied.

"A what?" DeAnna asked with laughter in her voice. "You are always makin' somethin'. Can I come over and see it?"

"No, you know my mother doesn't like me havin' company when she's not here," Shelly replied sternly. "But we could do our homework over the phone."

"How?" DeAnna asked.

"Ask me what do I eat or what fun things do I do in space, stuff like that," Shelly replied.

The two girls spent the next hour on the phone. DeAnna would ask questions about living in space and Shelly would answer. They decided that they would present their homework together. "Let's make this a play," Shelly said.

"Roger, Space Station, but we better write this stuff down so we don't forget it," DeAnna responded. "Can you bring your space station to class tomorrow?"

"I'd like to," Shelly responded. "But, I'll have to ask mom if she'll drive me to school 'cause I can't carry all of these boxes. DeAnna, bring your little brother's walkie talkies. And his sleeping bag too 'cause it's like the one the astronauts sleep in."

"Roger, Space Station. Can I help you put your station together?" DeAnna asked.

"Sure. I mean, Roger, Earth!" Shelly responded with laughter. "I gotta go. Mom will be home soon and I have to finish my homework."

"Roger, this is Earth to Space Station Shelly–Out!" DeAnna said in a commanding voice.

"Space Station Shelly to Earth–Out!" Shelly said, waving to her friend.

Try it Do the "My Personal Space Station" activity.

Age: 5 and Up
Time: 10 to 20 minutes

My Personal Space Station

Can you build a space station in your room?

Get it

4 or more cardboard boxes (medium or large)
Paper
Markers or crayons
Tape
Bed sheet or blanket

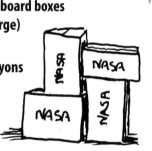

Read it

✓ Cardboard boxes can be collected from grocery stores, clothing stores, or bookstores.

✓ In step 2, ask the child to draw pictures for all four sides of each box. This will allow the child to rotate the boxes and change scenes.

✓ You may want to read "Shelly's Space Adventure" before doing the activity.

1. Help the child place the boxes on the floor in two rows.

2. Ask the child to draw pictures of what he thinks space would look like from the window of his space station. Tape the drawings to the sides of the boxes.

3. Lay a bed sheet or blanket over the boxes. Ask the child what he will need in space and have him place some of those items in the space station.

Try it

Add more boxes and make your station bigger.

Visit the library and get a book on space stations.

The Space Station Challenge. Write a letter to a friend describing your space station and telling her why she should visit you in space.

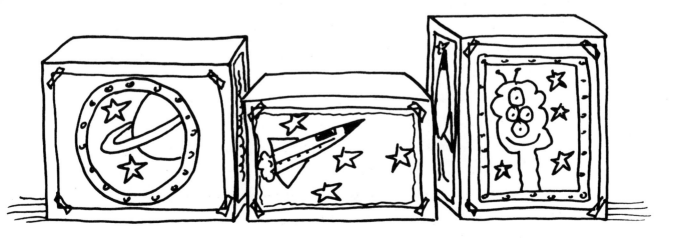

 *Think about it*

Did you know that the United States is working on a space station? They hope to send crew members into space to live in the space station. The crew members will perform experiments as well as continue to add living and working rooms. By the year 2000, crews from other nations will join the effort. The oxygen, water, and waste will be purified and reused. Only food will have to be resupplied from Earth to support human life. Did you know that the stations would have to carry dehydrated food, like the meals served on the space shuttle? Today, crew members can choose from more than 70 food items and 20 beverages. An example of the foods served are orange drink, peaches, eggs, sweet rolls, soup, ham and cheese, stewed tomatoes, and beefsteak. Years after the space station is completed, small vegetable gardens will provide fresh produce. The gardens will also help to absorb carbon dioxide from the space station's atmosphere while supplying oxygen for the crew.

Age: 6 and Up
Time: 10 to 20 minutes

Ships Ahoy

Can you make a boat that is powered by water?

Get it

Empty half-gallon milk or juice carton

Scissors

Ruler or tape measure

Paper cup

Tape or glue

Plastic straw (flexible straws work best)

Bathtub

Read it

✓ *If you want to try this activity with a child under age six, complete steps 1 through 3 before you do this activity with the child. If possible, make one or two extra boats.*

✓ *Make sure that the hole in the boat is near the bottom of the boat. Also, make the hole in the cup in step 3 at the same height as the hole in the boat so that all of the water will drain from the cup. (See illustration.)*

✓ *If your boat tips over, move the cup around until the boat becomes stable.*

Do it

1. Cut the carton lengthwise leaving the sides of the carton about three inches high all around. This will be the boat.

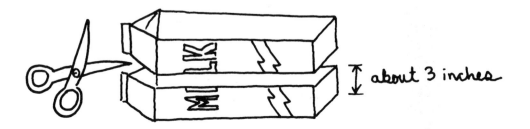

about 3 inches

Try it

Instead of using a cup, use a small carton. Watch what happens.

Add coins or paper clips to the boat and watch how it affects the speed of the boat as well as the boat's ability to float.

Have boat races and contests to see how many circles the boats can make and how far they will travel.

Do the "Wave Maker" activity.

The Ships Ahoy Challenge.
Punch three holes, one above the other, on one side of a plastic soda bottle. Cover the holes with tape and fill the bottle with water. Predict from which hole the water will travel the farthest. Hold the bottle over a sink, remove the tape, and watch what happens.

2. Make a small hole in the back of the carton. It should be just a little smaller than the width of the straw.

3. Make a hole in the side of the paper cup near the bottom. This hole should be level with the hole in the carton.

4. Glue or tape the cup in the boat. Before you glue the cup, make sure that the cup is properly balanced in the boat to prevent it from capsizing. Then slide the straw through the hole in the boat and the cup.

5. Fill the tub with a few inches of water and put the boat in it. Make sure that the part of the straw that extends from the boat is underwater.

6. Hold your finger over the end of the straw that is underwater. At the same time have the child fill the cup with water. Remove your finger and watch what happens.

7. Bend the straw left, right, up, and down and watch how the boat moves. What would happen if the straw were longer or shorter? What would happen if you used two straws or a bigger cup or did not use a cup and filled the carton with water?

Think about it

When you released the water from the straw, the boat started to move. It moved because the water near the bottom of the cup had the force of the water above it pushing it out. As a result, the water moving through the straw had a stronger force than the water around it. This force is one part of a concept of motion called "action and reaction," which played a major role in the boat moving. The concept of action and reaction means that for every action moving in one direction there is an equal reaction moving in the opposite direction. The water escaping through the straw pushed against the water in the tub, which was the action. The reaction was the water in the tub pushing back against the boat, which moved the boat forward. The size and direction of the straw affected the action, which in turn affected the reaction—how fast and in what direction the boat moved.

Age: 4 to 7
Time: 10 to 20 minutes

Slip and Slide

Can you slide across a variety of surfaces?

Get it

2 pairs of socks

2 medium-sized brown paper bags

String

Scissors

2 plastic garbage bags

Coin

Aluminum foil

Tape

Newspaper

Waxed paper

Cardboard

Ice cube

Read it

✓ Make sure the area is free of any breakable items, such as furniture and glass.

✓ Make sure the floor is free of splinters or sharp edges.

✓ Practice sliding on the floor with the child before you start the activity.

Do it

1. Help the child put on two pairs of socks and slide across a tile or wooden floor and then across a rug. Was she able to slide across any of the surfaces? Ask her to feel and describe the different surfaces.

2. Ask the child to place each foot in a medium-sized paper bag. Cut two pieces of string long enough to tie the bags to her legs. Ask her to slide on a tile or wooden floor and then on a rug. Was she able to slide better than when wearing just socks?

3. Keep the paper bags on her feet and have her step into two plastic garbage bags. Ask the child to slide across the different floor surfaces again. Did the garbage bags work better than the socks and the paper bags?

4. Remove all of the bags from the child's feet and go to a table. Tell the child that you are going to play a game of table hockey. Stand across from her and cup your hand to make a goal. Ask her to slide a coin across the table and into the goal. Did the coin slide?

Try it

Rub your hands together and time how long it takes before they get warm. Try it again, this time putting water, oil, or lotion on your hands before you rub them together. What happens?

The Slip and Slide Challenge.
Make an ice hockey board. Fill half of a shallow baking pan with water. Place a piece of yarn at both ends of the pan in the form of a goal, and freeze it (preferably overnight). Slide a coin across the icy surface to play hockey.

IT'S A GOAL!

5. Now tape a piece of aluminum foil across the width of the table. Ask the child to slide a coin across the aluminum foil into the goal. How did the coin move over the aluminum foil?

6. Place the following items on the table next to each other: newspaper, waxed paper, and cardboard. Slide the coin over these surfaces. Did the child score any goals?

7. Try scoring goals with an ice cube. Slide the ice cube across each of the surfaces. Did you score more goals using the ice cube or the coins?

Think about it

When you ran across the room, you used your feet to get you moving. Once you started sliding you slowed down and then stopped because of friction. Friction is what prevents things, like your feet, from sliding freely over another thing, like the floor. Friction also creates heat. The greater the friction, the greater the heat. When you put different objects, like socks or bags, on your feet you reduced the amount of friction. The reduction in friction caused you to slide farther. Water, like plastic bags, is another way to reduce friction. When the ice cube moved across the table, friction was created and the ice cube began to melt. The ice cube slid across a thin layer of water and not directly on the table, so the friction was greatly reduced.

Age: 3 to 7
Time: 15 minutes

Sounds Funny

MUNCH
CRUNCH
MUNCH

Can you identify food just by hearing it?

Get it

2 pieces of 5 different noisy foods such as carrots, celery, chips, and apples
Paper towel
Container

Read it

✓ *Make sure the child is not allergic to any of the foods chosen for this activity.*

Do it

1. Place five different noisy foods on a paper towel in front of the child. Place five more pieces of the same foods in a container for yourself.

2. Ask the child to close his eyes and listen to the sound of the food as you bite into it. Ask him to match the sound he heard to the food in front of him.

3. Continue until all of the food sounds have been identified. You may have to take another bite of a food if he has a difficult time identifying the sound.

4. Switch places. Let the child make the first sound and you try to match the food to the sound.

Try it

Sit inside or outside with your eyes closed, listen for different sounds, and try to identify what you hear.

Blindfold the child; click two coins together behind, beside, and over his head. Ask him to tell you the direction of the sound.

Cover a bowl with plastic and secure it with a rubber band. Sprinkle sugar on the plastic and clap your hands, yell, or hit a pan with a spoon next to the bowl to make the sugar dance.

The Sounds Funny Challenge.

Tape record your food sounds and write down which foods you bit into to make the sounds. Play the tape later and try to identify each sound.

5. Go on a noisy food scavenger hunt. What other noisy foods can the child find?

6. Create a funny sound for five foods that don't make a noise such as a banana and ice cream.

Think about it

Every time you eat, your food talks to or communicates with you through sound. When you bite into your food, sound vibrates against the air and the bones inside of your mouth. These vibrations move in waves. When you chew food, you hear most of the sounds from inside your head. The bones in your head carry the sounds to your eardrum. The eardrum is a thin membrane that vibrates like the skin on a drum. The eardrum passes the sounds to tiny bones deeper inside your ear. Finally, your nerves carry the message of the vibrations to your brain. Your brain tells you if the food is noisy or quiet. Your brain also identifies which food made the sound.

Age: 3 and Up
Time: 10 to 20 minutes

Spot the Patterns

How many patterns can you find in your home?

Get it

Pattern activity cards (provided on page 129)
Scissors
Tape
8 index cards

Read it

✓ *Trace or copy the pattern activity cards provided and tape them to index cards. This will make the cards more durable.*

1. Ask the child to look around the house and point out some of the patterns that she sees.

2. Give the child one of the activity cards. Help her find an object or item in her house that has the same pattern as her activity card.

3. Give the child the remaining cards and help her hunt for the patterns around the house.

Try it

Go on a pattern rubbing hunt. Take a white sheet of paper and several crayons around your house or neighborhood, and rub license plates, leaves, bricks, and so on.

Create works of art using pasta and string. Draw a pattern on an index card and re-create the pattern using an assortment of pasta and string.

Do the "Parade of Patterns" activity.

The Spot the Patterns Challenge.

Have the child hide while you search the room or house for a pattern to draw. Draw the pattern on a piece of paper, give it to the child, and ask her to find the pattern. Take turns hunting for the patterns.

4. Ask the child to give you the cards and watch you look for other items with patterns that match the cards.

 **Think about it**

Patterns can be found everywhere in our environment. We can observe patterns in the leaves of a tree, in the cracks in a sidewalk, in grains of wood, and in fabrics in our clothing. There are so many types of patterns that once you pay attention to patterns around you it's hard to find objects that don't have a pattern in them. Finding patterns is the way our brain makes sense of the world.

pattern activity cards

Age: 5 and Up
Time: 10 to 20 minutes

Stacks of Fun

BEST IN SHOW

Can you build a work of art using paper?

Get it

Multicolored construction paper

Tape

Table

5 small or light-weight books

Paper towel tubes

Cereal boxes

Paper cups

Piece of paper

Read it

✓ If you want to do this activity with a child who is younger than five, do steps 1 through 3 before starting the activity with the child.

COOL!

130

Do it

1. Help the child fold a sheet of construction paper into thirds, open it up, and tape the long edges of the paper together to make a triangle.

2. Help the child fold a second sheet of construction paper in half. Open it up and fold the halves in half. Tape the long edges of the paper together to form a rectangle.

3. Roll a sheet of construction paper into a tube and tape it so it remains a tube.

4. Stand the paper shapes up on a table. Ask the child to carefully place a small book on each one of the shapes. Will all of the shapes hold one book? Add a second book to each shape. Which shape held the most books?

5. Try this! Place a book on the triangular shape. Then place the rectangular shape on top of the book and continue stacking the paper and the books. You may want to make more shapes. How high can you build it? What would happen if you used all tubular shapes? Does it matter if the books are different weights?

6. Build a tower with the following items: paper towel tubes, cereal boxes, and paper cups. Keep in mind that the higher the structure, the less stable it will become. To test the stability of your tower, stomp your feet or wave a piece of paper in front of your structure. Did your structure fall?

Try it

Build structures with cards, building blocks, or dominoes.

Make a structure using coins. Stack 50 pennies without them falling. Try again with nickels or quarters, or use a mixture of coins. Determine which coins make the best structures.

Do the "Build a Better Chair" activity.

The Stacks of Fun Challenge. Collect at least five paper towel or toilet paper rolls. Cut two to four slits in each tube and stack the tubes by sliding them together. Build a structure that is tall, long, or both.

Think about it

When you folded the construction paper into shapes, you made it stronger. A structure that is tubular, like a paper cup or cardboard tube, is strong. It does not collapse easily because the sides of the tube are rigid. Once you created a strong base you were able to build higher. Each tube could support only a certain amount of weight, so you had to expand the bottom in order to balance all of the weight on top. You had to make sure that your structure was balanced. Objects with wide bases, like towers, have a low center of gravity, which makes them more stable and prevents them from falling over. The "Keep Your Balance" activity will tell you more about this. The construction paper shapes were able to support the weight of the small books because the weight was shared or distributed. This means that all sides of the paper supported the book and no one part of the paper carried all the weight.

Age: 3 to 5
Time: 10 to 20 minutes

Stretch It Out

Can you stretch an object out of shape?

Get it

Collect three of the following stretchable objects: balloon, clay, clothes with elastic bands (pants, sweatshirts, headband), suspenders, bed sheets, sponge

Pencil

Old pair of nylon stockings

Rubber gloves

Aluminum foil

20 pennies

2 rubber bands

Scissors

Paper cup

String

Paper clip

Read it

✓ *Make sure the child never points the rubber bands toward anyone's eyes.*

✓ *If an object doesn't stretch easily, don't force it.*

Do it

1. Ask the child to help you collect and place three stretchable objects on the floor. Give the child a pencil and ask him to try to stretch it. Then ask him to do the same thing with the remaining three objects he collected. Did anything happen?

2. Ask the child to grab one end of the nylon stockings as you grab the other. How far will one of the legs stretch? Let go of both ends. What happened to the stockings? Will the rubber gloves stretch as far as the stockings?

3. Tear off a sheet of aluminum foil large enough to wrap 20 pennies into a tight ball. Cut and tie a rubber band around the ball of aluminum foil. Hold the rubber band and ask the child to pull the ball down without breaking the rubber band. How far will it stretch? What happens if he releases the ball?

4. Punch two holes opposite each other near the rim of the paper cup. Tie a string though the hole to make a handle. Hook the paper clip around the middle of the string. Now hook a rubber band to the paper clip and hang it from a doorknob. Ask the child to fill the cup with pennies. How far will the cup stretch? What happens when he takes the pennies out of the cup?

Try it

The Stretch It Out Challenge.
Cut a big hole in the side and a small hole in the top of an empty milk carton. Hook a paper clip through the hole in the top and attach a rubber band to the paper clip. Loop the rubber band over a strong tree branch and fill the carton with bird seed. Watch your bird feeder and see if it will be strong enough to support the weight of the seed and the bird.

5. Look around the house for five more stretchy objects. Can you find five objects that will not stretch?

 *Think about it*

When you stretched the objects and let them go, one of two things happened. They stayed stretched or they returned to their original shapes. If the objects sprang back, they had elasticity. An object can only be stretched by applying a force, like pulling, and can only be stretched a certain distance. When you applied more force, one of two things happened. The object broke or remained stretched. When you stretch an object, it is under stress. All solids are made up of atoms. The atoms are held together by bonds, which are like springs. When the object is stressed, the atoms are pulled apart. This means that the bonds were stretched. When the stress is released, the atoms either spring back or remain pulled apart. Rubber bands are made of a very elastic material that stretches easily. This is because its atoms are arranged in long molecules that are coiled like springs. The rubber band's molecules can uncoil when stretched and recoil when released.

Taster's Choice

Can you identify foods as solids or liquids just by tasting them?

Get it

Blindfold
3 slices of fruits or vegetables
3 paper cups

Juice or juice boxes to match the fruit or vegetable slices (orange/orange juice, apple/apple juice, carrot/carrot juice)
Blender

Read it

✓ Ask a parent if there are any fruits or vegetables the child may not eat. Also, ask if you may use a blender.

✓ For the purposes of this activity explain that a solid is hard and a liquid is wet.

✓ Step 5 asks you to freeze a cup of juice or a juice box. Freeze the box before starting the activity or overnight.

✓ Use a microwave on the defrost setting or put the box in a bowl of hot water for a few minutes to soften a frozen juice box.

I KNOW WHAT IT IS!

ORANGE

ORANGE JUICE

Do it

1. Blindfold the child. Give her one slice of fruit and the juice that matches. Ask the child to identify the type of fruit and drink. Remove the blindfold and ask her to point to the solid and then the liquid.

Try it

• • • • • • • • • • • • • • • •

Experiment with cooking oil, milk, and water. Which item will freeze the fastest? Will they all freeze?

Make a batch of your favorite fruit punch, pour it into ice trays, and freeze. Add the ice cubes to your favorite drink.

Place an ice cube in a bowl and add salt. What happens?

Do the "Nosy Detective" activity.

The Taster's Choice Challenge. Determine if an egg is a solid, liquid, or both. Carefully break open an egg onto a plate and answer these questions: Is the eggshell a solid or liquid? Is the clear membrane around the yolk (the yellow part) a solid or liquid? Break the membrane. Is the yolk a solid or liquid? If you boil an egg, is it a solid or liquid?

2. Repeat step 1 for the remaining slices of fruit and cups of juice.

3. Find three more solids. Ask the child if a solid can be turned into a liquid.

4. Place a slice of fruit or vegetable in the blender. Liquefy the solid, pour it in a glass, and let the child taste it. Ask the child what happened to the solid.

5. Ask the child if a liquid can be turned into a solid. Give the child the frozen drink box and a straw. Ask her to put the straw into the box and drink the juice. What happened?

6. Suggest warming the box up. Help the child find two or three different ways to turn the solid into a liquid.

Think about it

All things, including foods, are made up of atoms. The closer the atoms are to each other the slower they move. We refer to them as solids. Heat is needed to move the atoms apart. When you heat a solid, it gives the atoms energy. They start vibrating and moving away from each other. This causes solids to melt when you heat them. The blender forced the atoms to move past each other, which produced heat. The atoms in a liquid are not so close together and are moving faster than in a solid. When the liquid was introduced to cold air the atoms slowed down, produced less heat, and clung together to form a solid. When something goes from a solid to a liquid and back we refer to this as a change in its state. Your ability to taste foods relies on the use of the taste buds on your tongue. Each taste bud has many taste cells, which are surrounded by nerve fibers. As food starts to dissolve on your tongue, the food releases chemicals. These chemicals were detected by the nerves, which sent a signal to your brain. Your brain told you if the food was a solid or liquid.

Age: 4 to 8
Time: 10 to 20 minutes

That's Attractive

Can you make drops of water act like magnets?

Waxed paper

2 spray bottles

Water

Food coloring (2 colors)

Straw

Spoon

Coin

Pen

 Read *it*

✓ *If you do not have spray bottles then fill two small bowls with water and add food coloring. Dip your hands in the water and lightly shake the water onto the waxed paper.*

1. Tear off two sheets of waxed paper about 12 inches long. Place the paper on a flat surface with the waxed or shiny side up.

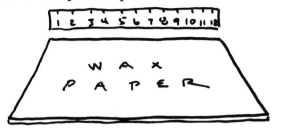

2. Fill the spray bottles with water and add one of the food colorings to each bottle—the darker the color the better. Spray water onto one sheet of waxed paper.

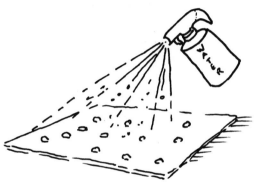

3. Give the child a straw and ask him to blow the water droplets together until they form one big raindrop.

Try it

Punch three holes, side by side, in the bottom of a plastic bottle. Cover the holes while filling the bottle with water in a sink. Uncover the holes, pinch the streams of water together, and watch what happens.

Blow up a balloon and rub it through your hair. Now, hold the balloon over a handful of ripped-up paper or puffed rice. What happens?

The That's Attractive Challenge. Run a comb through your hair and then hold it vertically next to a very thin stream of flowing water.

COOL!

4. On the second sheet of waxed paper, spray both colors. Separate the colors into two piles by moving the water drops with some of the following household objects: a spoon, a coin, and a pen. Place one end of each item halfway into a drop of water and slowly pull the water drop toward another drop.

5. Find five more items that can be used to move the water drops around. Did you find any items that couldn't move the water?

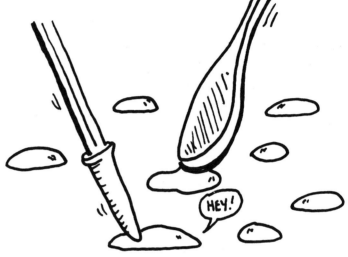

Think about it

Each drop of water is made of atoms that have positive and negative charges that form molecules, which are groups of atoms. These molecules have one side that is more negatively charged and another side that is more positively charged. The negatively charged end of one water molecule is attracted to the positively charged end of another water molecule. Positive and negative charges attract or pull together. The attractive force among water molecules is called a cohesive force. It is this attraction that causes the drops of water to pull together. When you placed the pen in the water drop, the water was attracted to the negative charges in the pen. Attraction between two different materials like a pen and water is called an adhesive force.

Age: 5 and Up
Time: 10 to 20 minutes

Total Dizziness

Can you play simple games while you are dizzy?

Get it

Ball

Frisbee or a round plastic lid

Read it

✓ This activity should be played outside.

✓ We want the child to have fun and not get hurt or sick. Play in the grass so the child can move around safely. Keep away from toys, trees, rocks, buildings, and cars.

✓ Also, make sure that the child takes breaks. If the child ever complains of feeling sick, stop immediately and have her rest for a while.

Do it

1. Stand a few feet away from the child. Practice throwing and kicking a ball to each other, walking toward each other in a straight line, and tossing a Frisbee. Do each task a couple of times. Also, try these tasks: touch your nose with your pointing finger and close one eye while picking up the ball.

Try it

1. **Blindfold the child and spin her around five times and stop.** Ask her to point in the direction she thinks she is moving (clockwise or counter clockwise).

2. **Spin the child around five times with her eyes closed and stop.** Ask her to open her eyes. Watch the movements that her eyes are making. Reverse roles so she can watch your eyes.

3. **Spin the child around five times with her eyes open and stop.** Ask the child to locate the same object, like a tree or a picture, each time she spins around.

   Which of the three ways she spun made her feel the least dizzy?

The Total Dizziness Challenge. Do the "Keep Your Balance" activity.

2. Spin around five times and then try to throw or kick the ball. Now spin around five more times and try to walk in a straight line. Have the child do the same. Was it easy to perform each task? How did you feel?

3. With your eyes open, take turns spinning each other around five times and perform the tasks listed in step 1.

4. Find three other tasks to perform. Make sure that the tasks are safe. Experiment with closing one or both of your eyes before and after spinning. Did it make a difference?

Think about it

You spun around. You got dizzy. You got dizzy because of the fluid (liquid) that is in the semicircular canal located in your inner ear. The fluid changes position or moves whenever you move your head. Inside the canals are tiny hairs that are connected to nerves. These nerves tell your brain whether the fluid is moving and in which direction. Your brain uses this information to judge whether or not you are moving. Too much movement of the fluid in your ears, however, caused you to feel dizzy. You continued to feel dizzy after you stopped turning because the fluid continued to move for a short period of time.

Age: 7 and Up
Time: 10 to 20 minutes

Total Recall

Can you remember everything that you see?

 Get it

Collect these 10 or similar objects: toothbrush, coin, spoon, pencil, small book, playing card, small toy, ruler, scissors, paper clip

10 more items

Table

Towel (large enough to completely cover all 10 objects)

 Read it

✓ If you don't have all of the items listed above, make substitutions.

✓ If you want to try this activity with a child younger than seven, then start with three objects and then add three or more objects.

 Do it

1. Ask the child to hide in another room while you place all of the objects on a table and cover them with the towel.

DON'T PEEK!

2. Call the child and ask him to sit in front of the covered objects. Remove the towel and ask him to study the objects for 30 seconds. Cover the items again and ask him to recall as many objects as possible.

3. Remove the towel and ask him to count the items he recalled. Did he forget any? Now let the child collect and cover 10 new items and you try to recall them. How did you do?

I FORGOT THAT ONE...

TAH DA!

Try it

Close your eyes and recall the total number of windows, doors, or light switches in your house.

The Total Recall Challenge.
Place five or more objects (books, toys, and so on) on the ground in an *S* pattern. Make sure that there is about three feet between the objects. Ask the child to memorize the placement of each object by walking around them a few times. Now, blindfold the child and ask him to walk around each object without touching it.

4. What would happen if you related the object to its purpose? For example, I fix my hair with the brush, a toothbrush cleans my teeth, and I cut paper with the scissors. Do you think that this would help you remember more? Try this with a couple of the items that you collected. Was it easier?

5. Let's make things harder! Let the child look at one side of a penny for 15 to 30 seconds. Now hide the coin and ask the child to draw the penny with as much detail as possible. Compare the drawing to the coin. What did he recall?

Think about it

Why do we forget? Our brain gets so much information that it tries to put it all into one of two storage containers. Everything starts out being put into the container called "short-term memory." Short-term memory is where a small amount of new information, like the names in the "Total Recall" activity, sits for a couple of seconds or hours before being transferred to the other storage container, "long-term memory." Long-term memory is where information that we will need forever is stored. Because short-term memory can hold only so much information, old information gets bumped out by newer information. During the activity your brain had to quickly store all of the different objects you were looking at into short-term memory. You kept forcing new information in and some old information got bumped out of the way. That's why you forgot some things. Very little, if any, of the information was ever transferred to long-term memory.

Age: 7 and Up
Time: 20 to 30 minutes

Totally Tubular

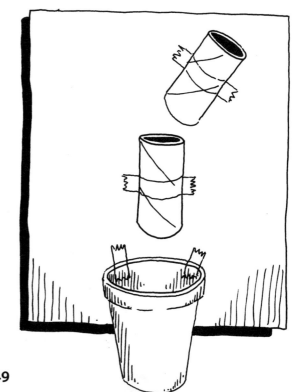

WHEEEE

> *Can you build a roller coaster maze out of tubes and cups?*

Get it

Piece of cardboard about the size of a TV screen

Tape

2 paper cups with the bottoms cut out

5 cardboard tubes such as paper towel tubes, wrapping paper tubes, or toilet paper tubes

Marble (or ball similar in size)

Scissors

Read it

✓ Make sure the child uses safety scissors.

✓ Try this activity before doing it with a child so you can make creative suggestions and give helpful hints.

✓ Make sure the child does not put the marble or ball in her mouth.

B.

A.

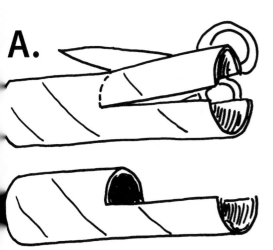

Do it

1. Tape the piece of cardboard against a vertical surface like a wall. Place the cups and tubes on the floor so the child can see what she has to work with.

2. Help the child tape a paper cup to the bottom of the piece of cardboard. Tape a cardboard tube above the cup (see diagram B). Ask her to roll the marble through the tube. Does the marble make it into the cup? If it missed, what can you do to make the marble roll into the cup?

3. Assist the child with taping a second tube to the piece of cardboard. Does the marble roll through both tubes and into the cup without stopping? If the marble stopped, what caused it to stop? How can you make it roll into the cup?

4. Now, add more tubes and cups. Cut the tubes to different lengths. See how many twists and curves you can put in your maze. Can you make the marble roll up a hill? Does the marble go all the way through your maze? Does it get stuck anywhere? Can you make one of the mazes from the diagrams provided?

CUT OPEN ← BOTTOM OF CUP

Try it

Lay a cardboard tube at an angle off the edge of a book. Roll a marble through it and time how long it takes to roll out. Add more books to increase the angle. Determine what makes the marble roll faster or slower. Use this information to create a faster-moving maze.

Build a tube maze down a flight of stairs.

The Totally Tubular Challenge. Construct a double-sided maze! Cut a hole in the top right of a cardboard square and a second hole in the bottom left. Construct a maze that allows a marble to roll from one side of the maze to the other (see illustration to the right). You will need to cut two tubes (see diagram A). This will help catch the marble as it drops behind the cardboard.

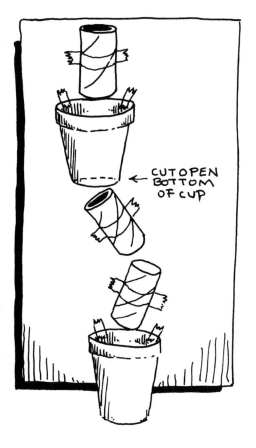

CUTOPEN
BOTTOM
OF CUP

5. Build a maze that makes the marble roll across the floor and into a cup. Build a ramp for the marble to jump over. Did it work?

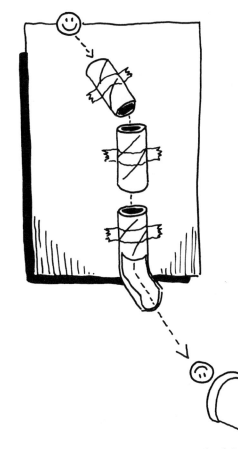

Think about it

The marble rolled through the maze because several things occurred. First, gravity, a force that pulls things to the Earth, helped the marble roll down through the maze. Second, you had to attach each tube at a downward slope so that the marble would roll. Changing the degree of the slope increased or decreased the speed of the marble. Finally, energy started the marble rolling. The marble used stored, or potential, energy and working, or kinetic, energy. When you picked the marble up, it was ready to work or had the potential to do work, in this case to roll. When you released the marble, it started rolling through the tubes or working. When objects roll down an incline, their potential or stored energy changes into kinetic or working energy.

WHEEEE!

Age: 3 and Up
Time: 10 to 20 minutes

Wave Maker

Can you make waves using household materials?

Get it

Towels and bath mats

Bathtub

Toy that floats such as a small plastic ball

Wave makers such as rubber spatulas, wire whisks, plastic spoons, and a ruler

Watch or clock

Rubber band

Read it

✓ *This is a great bath-time activity.*

✓ *If you have difficulty seeing the waves in the tub then add liquid soap or bubble bath.*

✓ *This activity can get messy, so be patient and prepared.*

1. This is a fun and wet activity. Be sure to lay the bath mats down before starting the activity. Place all of your wave making items by the bathtub.

2. Put water in the bathtub so it is one-third filled. Have the child place his hands underwater and then move his hands back and forth quickly and then slowly. Ask him to move his hands with his fingers spread apart and with his fingers together. Identify which movements produced the largest waves without splashing water out of the bathtub.

3. Drop a toy into the water. Did it make waves? What did the child notice about the waves? For example, were the waves small? Did they move slowly? in which direction did they move?

4. Ask the child to make big and small waves using the remaining wave makers. Find one item that makes the best waves.

5. Using your wave makers, push the toy to the other side of the tub (without actually touching the toy). Time how long it takes to accomplish this task. Will large waves move the toy faster than smaller waves? Does splashing move the boat forward?

6. Create five more ways to make great waves. Cut and stretch a rubber band so part of it is underwater. Ask the child to pluck it. What happens to the rubber band and the water?

Try it

Do the "Ships Ahoy" activity and then combine it with this activity.

The Wave Maker Challenge.

Using a ball or toy that floats and a bathtub, you and the child must push the floating object to the opposite end of the tub without actually touching the object. Your hands have to be underwater at all times.

foooo

Think about it

When you disturbed the water by pushing or pulling it with your hand, the water molecules either moved toward or away from your hand. When you dropped the ball into the water, the water molecules moved away from the ball in all directions. The rings that you saw were produced by vibrating molecules. Like sound waves, water produces waves of molecules that move to and fro, producing energy. The energy is what we see or refer to as waves. Dropping items into the bathtub did produce waves but did not create a force great enough to move your toy. But when you moved your hands or the spatula back and forth under the water, you produced two things. First, you produced waves which were visible, on the surface of the water. Second, you produced a current, which was not visible, under the water. It was the current of moving water that pulled the toy along, not the waves. Waves are up and down movements of water, and currents are side to side or horizontal movements.

Age: 5 and Up
Time: 10 to 20 minutes

Weather Patterns

Can you predict when the sun will shine again?

Get it

Weather cards (provided on page 158)
Weather section of a newspaper

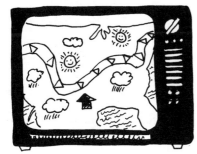

Read it

✓ Make four photocopies of the weather cards provided and cut out all of the cards before starting the activity. If you cannot make photocopies of the weather cards, then place a piece of white paper over the cards and trace them with a pencil.

✓ If the child has difficulty with patterns, try the "Spot the Patterns" activity first.

✓ If your newspaper does not have a weather section then watch the weather forecast on the news or videotape it.

Do it

1. Place the weather cards on the floor. Make a pattern using three cards (for example, sun, rain, sun). Ask the child to find the weather cards that match and duplicate the pattern. Make two more patterns for the child to duplicate. How did she do?

2. Make a pattern but leave one of the cards out (for example, sun, _____, sun). Ask the child to complete the pattern. Create two more patterns and then let the child make a few. How did she do?

3. Make your patterns longer. Use four to seven cards to make a pattern that the child must duplicate (sun, rain, sun, rain, sun). Using the same pattern, remove one or two cards and ask the child to find the missing card(s) and fill in the pattern.

4. Let the child make her own patterns. Can you duplicate her patterns? Can you find the card(s) missing from her patterns? How did you do?

Try it

Look through the newspaper and find weather patterns for different cities (for example, Washington, D.C. had rain on Monday and Tuesday and sun on Wednesday).

Write a weather poem or short story. Or go to the library and read a child's book that talks about weather.

Do the "Blown Away" activity.

The Weather Patterns Challenge.

Using a blank calendar, predict the weather for the first seven days. Draw a weather picture for each day. For example, draw rain on Monday and Tuesday and sun on Wednesday. Place the weather pattern cards provided in a bag and shake them up. Select a card and place the card next to the first day on the calendar. Repeat this for each day and see how many matches you have.

5. Show the child the weather section of the newspaper. Show her the pictures or icons that represent the weather. Explain that there are people called meteorologists who study the weather and predict what the weather will be each day. Can you find any weather icons that match your cards?

6. Pick out the weather cards that correspond to yesterday, today, and tomorrow's weather.

Think about it

Monday and Tuesday rain, Wednesday sun, Thursday and Friday ... ? What's up with the weather? Well, the answer is all around you. Weather is produced by warm air that rises, cools, and falls back to Earth. The air holds tiny drops of water. Warm air holds more water drops than cold air, so when the warm air cools, raindrops form. When the drops freeze, they become snow, ice, or hail. Wait. That's not all air does! It also produces wind and clouds. All of this happens every day and that's how weather patterns form.

LOOK WHAT THEY'VE PREDICTED...

weather cards

Age: 3 to 5
Time: 10 to 20 minutes

Where Do I Go?

Can you help Robby Robin find his family?

 Get it

Shapes (provided on page 162)

Construction paper

Pencil

Scissors

Paste or glue

3 pieces of white paper

Ruler

Crayons or markers

 Read it

✓ Before starting this activity with the child, trace the shapes onto sheets of construction paper and cut them out. You will need six large circles, six small circles, six large ovals, six small ovals, seven large triangles, and 14 small triangles.

Do it

1. Read the following story to the child:

Once upon a time, there was a bird named Robby. He lived with his family in a nest high in the treetops. One day, Robby and his family decided to spend the day flying, since the sun was shining and the sky was clear. As they were flying, Robby started daydreaming. All of a sudden, he realized he had lost his family. Robby needs you to help him find his family.

2. Help the child paste six large circles in a line near the bottom of a piece of white paper. Paste each of the six small circles about one-inch above each large circle.

3. Ask the child to draw legs extending from the six large circles and then draw necks and faces on the six small circles. Now you have a row of ostriches! Draw grass and the sky with a couple of clouds.

4. Read this to the child:

As Robby was searching for his family, he met the Ostrich family. "Hi!" Robby said. "I'm looking for my family. We were out flying today, and I lost my way." Olive Ostrich said, "We aren't your family, because we can't fly. There is a family of birds around the corner. Why don't you ask them?"

5. Help the child paste six large ovals in a line near the bottom portion of a second sheet of white paper. Then paste each of the six small ovals to the top of each large oval.

6. Next, ask the child to draw a face on each of the small ovals and wings on each of the large ovals to form a line of ducks. Draw water, a sky, and some clouds to complete the picture.

7. Read this to the child:

Robby walked up to the family and said, "I'm looking for my family. I was flying with them and I lost my way." Delores Duck said to

Try it

Create pictures using different shapes. Simply cut out different shapes, paste them to paper, and use markers or crayons to decorate each shape. Try using two different shapes in your picture. Now, make up a story to go with your picture. It's fun! You can *Do It!*

Do the "Parade of Patterns" activity.

The Robby Robin Challenge. Create a story about Robby Robin searching for food. Make three scenes: 1) Robby meets a family of caterpillars, 2) he meets a family of beetles, and 3) he meets a family of worms. Use different shapes to create the families.

Robby, *"Where do you live?"* Robby replied, *"In a nest, high in the treetops!"* Delores said, *"I'm sorry, we live in a nest on the ground. Why don't you fly a little farther up the road? I saw a family of birds resting on a picket fence."*

8. Ask the child to paste six large triangles in a line in the middle of the third piece of paper. Now, have him paste a small triangle along both sides of each large triangle. Draw legs under the large triangles and faces near the top so the shapes turn into robins. Ask him to draw a fence for the birds to sit on, grass, and a sun or clouds.

9. Read this to the child:

As Robby approached the birds on the fence, he heard one of them yell, "Robby Robin, there you are!"

10. Help the child add one more bird to the fence using the extra triangular pieces. You have helped Robby find his family!

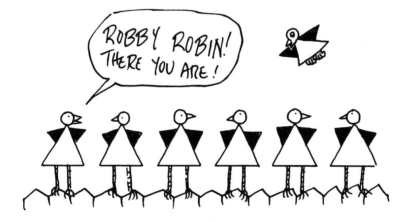

Think about it

You used patterns to help Robby find his family. Each family of birds that Robby met was made from different shapes. When you put the shapes in a row, you formed a pattern. Patterns are formed when things, like shapes, are repeated. The more complex the shapes and the greater the number used, the more complex the patterns formed.

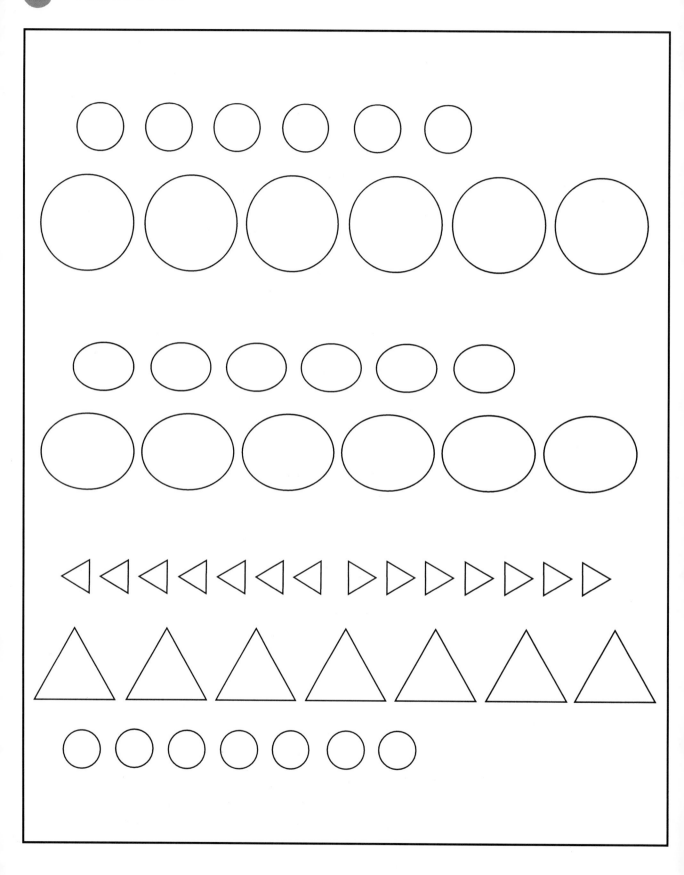

Age: 5 and Up
Time: 10 to 20 minutes

Zany Patterns

Can you turn cups into a game where you create patterns?

Get it

6 Styrofoam cups
Markers
2 straws (optional)

Read it

✓ Crayons can be substituted for the markers, but they may make holes in the cups.
✓ Markers may rub off on the child's fingers.

Do it

1. Turn one cup upside down on the floor. Draw a face on the cup. Place straws in the top of the cup to create antennae.

2. Draw a different shape on each of the remaining cups (for example, stars, circles, and so on).

3. Spread the cups out in a single line to create a caterpillar with patterns. Rearrange the cups to create a caterpillar with a new pattern. How many different patterns can you create?

4. Stack all of the cups together and set them upside down on a table. Draw a shape, like a square, on the lip of the top cup. Draw the same shape on the lip of the remaining cups. There should be a line of squares drawn down the stack of cups.

5. Draw another shape next to the square on the lip of the top cup. Leave space between each shape. Continue drawing shapes around the lip of the top cup until you run out of room. Remember, the patterns drawn on the top cup must be repeated on the rest of the cups. Make your shapes fun! Use eyes, noses, mouths, letters, numbers, and so on.

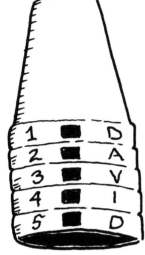

Try it

Use stickers instead of markers to make your zany patterns.

Go to a craft store and purchase plastic eyes, noses, and anything else you want. Glue them to the lips of each cup.

Do the "Spot the Patterns" and "Betcha Can't Find It!" activities.

The Zany Patterns Challenge.
Stack several cups together and write a message on them, similar to the way you drew the shapes on the cups, with one letter on each cup. Make sure each word is a different color. Give the cup to a friend and let her try to unscramble the message by matching the colors.

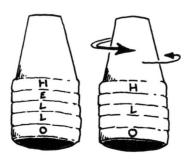

6. Place one hand inside the bottom cup and use your other hand to turn the top cup. If you push down lightly on the top cup, you can turn all of the cups at the same time, creating different patterns.

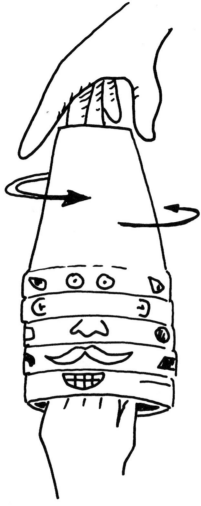

Think about it

When you drew shapes on the cups and lined them up, you created a pattern. When you moved the cups around, you created new patterns. Our ability to see a pattern is based on our ability to see something repeated. Simple patterns have simple repetitions. Complex patterns involve complex repetitions.

Acknowledgments

The ScienceMinders project, whose staff developed this activity book, had the assistance of many individuals to make it happen. Through the various stages, ScienceMinders had generous volunteers who gave numerous hours testing activities and implementing programs using the activities. Testing of materials for the book was undertaken by the following students, teachers, and child care programs with financial support from the National Science Foundation.

Special thanks to the activity testers including the students in the 1994 enrichment programs at the following schools: Annapolis Middle School, Annapolis, MD; Bates Middle School, Annapolis, MD; Magothy Middle School, Severna Park, MD; Key School, Annapolis, MD; and Southern Middle School, Lothian, MD. Thanks to teachers at Murch Elementary School, Washington, D.C.; students at Thomas Johnson Middle School, Bowie, MD; and the following child care programs: Wee Lad and Lassie, Arnold, MD; Severna Park Children's Center, Severna Park, MD; Children's Discovery Center, Columbia, MD; Children's Discovery Center, Severna Park, MD; Lake Arbor Child Care, Mitchellville, MD; Heritage Academy, Alexandria, VA; Kids First, Washington, D.C.; KidStop, Rockville, MD; and Primary Prep, Owings Mills, MD. Thanks also to the families in Maryland; Washington, D.C.; Virginia; and North Carolina who spent hours testing and evaluating activities.

We thank the Carnegie Science Center in Pittsburgh, PA, and the following YWCAs for participating in testing at a national level: Metropolitan Chicago; McKeesport, PA; El Paso, TX; Marion/Grant, IN; Greater Rhode Island; Harbor Area, CA; Hazelton, PA; White Plains and Central Westchester, NY; Downtown Lorain, OH; Shiawassee County, MI; Springfield, IL; and Waukesha, WI.

Thank you to our advisory committee consisting of scientists, mathematicians, and early childhood specialists who helped to check the accuracy of statements and the appropriateness of the activities in the book. In particular we would like to thank Maria Marable; Lynn Dierking, Ph.D.; Jamie Harms, M.D.; Sammy Epstein, Ph.D.; Elisa L. Klein, Ph.D.; Julie Dunbar; Jack Pettit; Judy Bender; and Marilyn Lamb.

Special thanks to Joan Cottle, who helped us get started with her wonderful illustrations; Aubrey Hill and Susan Schulz, two dynamic people and activity developers who brought sunshine and added life to the project; Sarah Greene, for her timely contribution to the selection of activities; and Becky Fye for helping with formative evaluation.

Finally, we would like to thank the YWCA of Annapolis and Anne Arundel County; Science Learning, Inc.; ScienceMinders codirector Pat Roche; and our families for being sounding boards, idea generators, and cheering sections.

Kids' Activity Books the Whole Family Can Enjoy

Big Book of Fun
Creative Learning Activities for Home & School, Ages 4–12
Carolyn Buhai Haas
Illustrated by Jane Bennet Phillips
Includes more than 200 projects and activities–from indoor-outdoor games and nature crafts to holiday ideas, cooking fun, and much more.
ISBN 1-55652-020-4
288 pages, paper, $11.95

Frank Lloyd Wright for Kids
Kathleen Thorne-Thomsen
A thorough biography is followed by stimulating projects that enable kids to grasp the ideas underlying Wright's work–and have fun in the process.
ages 8 & up
ISBN 1-55652-207-X
144 pages, paper, $14.95

Green Thumbs
A Kid's Activity Guide to Indoor and Outdoor Gardening
Laurie Carlson
With a few seeds, some water and soil, and this book, kids will be creating gardens of their own in no time. They will also create compost, make watering cans, mix up bug sprays, lay slug traps, grow crazy cucumbers, and much more.
ages 3–9
ISBN 1-55652-238-X
144 pages, paper, $12.95

Happy Birthday, Grandma Moses
Activities for Special Days Throughout the Year
Clare Bonfanti Braham and Maria Bonfanti Esche
Illustrated by Mary Jones
The significance of 100 different celebratory days is thoroughly explained as 200 related activities pay charming, educational tribute to the holidays, history, and accomplishments of many cultures and many people.
ages 3–9
ISBN 1-55652-226-6
304 pages, paper, $14.95

Huzzah Means Hooray
Activities from the Days of Damsels, Jesters, and Blackbirds in a Pie
Laurie Carlson
Kids can re-create a long-ago world of kings, castles, jousts, jesters, magic fairies, and Robin Hood–all they need are their imaginations and materials they can find at home.
ages 3–9
ISBN 1-55652-227-4
184 pages, paper, $12.95

Kids Camp!
Activities for the Backyard or Wilderness
Laurie Carlson and Judith Dammel
Young campers will build an awareness of the environment, learn about insect and animal behavior, boost their self-esteem, and acquire all the basic skills for fun, successful camping.
ages 4–12
ISBN 1-55652-237-1
176 pages, paper, $12.95

Look at Me
Creative Learning Activities for Babies and Toddlers
Carolyn Buhai Haas
Illustrated by Jane Bennett Phillips
Activities for babies and toddlers that inspire creativity and learning through play.
ISBN 1-55652-021-2
232 pages, paper, $11.95

Messy Activities and More
Virginia K. Morin
Illustrated by David Sokoloff
Foreword by Ann M. Jernberg
Encourages adults and children to have fun making a mess with more than 160 interactive games and projects.
ages 3–10
ISBN 1-55652-173-1
144 pages, paper, $9.95

More Than Moccasins
A Kid's Activity Guide to Traditional North American Indian Life
Laurie Carlson
Kids will discover traditions and skills handed down from the people who first settled this continent, including how to plant a garden, make useful pottery, and communicate through Navajo codes.

"As an educator who works with Indian children, I highly recommend [More Than Moccasins] for all kids and teachers. . . . I learned things about our Indian world I did not know."
—Bonnie Jo Hunt
Wicahpi Win (Star Woman)
Standing Rock Lakota
ages 3–9
ISBN 1-55652-213-4
200 pages, paper, $12.95

My Own Fun
Creative Learning Activities for Home and School
Carolyn Buhai Haas and Anita Cross Friedman
More than 160 creative learning projects and activities for elementary school children.
ages 7–12
ISBN 1-55652-093-X
208 pages, paper, $9.95

Pun and Games
Jokes, Riddles, Rhymes, Daffynitions, Tairy Fales, and More Wordplay for Kids
Richard Lederer
Illustrated by Dave Morice
Introduces the wacky world of wordplay with puns of every stripe, spoonerisms, games of word substition, and more. These will intrigue the young verbal acrobat and bamboozle teachers and parents who are not on their toes.
ages 10 & up
ISBN 1-55652-264-9
112 pages, paper, $9.95

Sandbox Scientist
Real Science Activities for Little Kids
Michael E. Ross
Illustrated by Mary Anne Lloyd
Parents, teachers, and day care leaders learn to assemble "Explorer Kits" that will send kids off on their own investigations, in groups or individually, with a minimum of adult intervention.
ages 2–8
ISBN 1-55652-248-7
208 pages, paper, $12.95

Shaker Children
True Stories and Crafts
Kathleen Thorne-Thomsen
This charming book combines two true biographies and authentic activities to tell children of today about the Shakers of yesterday.
ages 8 & up
ISBN 1-55652-250-9
128 pages, paper, $15.95

Splish Splash
Water Fun for Kids
Penny Warner

Kids love water—whether it's the ocean, lake, pool, or backyard sprinkler. Here are more than 120 ideas for water fun for toddlers to teens.
ages 2–12
ISBN 1-55652-262-2
172 pages, paper, $12.95

Westward Ho!
An Activity Guide to the Wild West
Laurie Carlson

Cowboys and cowgirls explore the West with activities such as sewing a sunbonnet, panning for gold, cooking flapjacks, singing cowboy songs, and much, much more.
ages 5–12
ISBN 1-55652-271-1
184 pages, paper, $12.95

Why Design?
Projects from the National Building Museum
Anna Slafer and Kevin Cahill

Containing photographs, illustrations, work sheets, and lists of questions for more than 40 projects, this book will stimulate anyone interested in design. Instructions on technical skills and special advice for educators is included, too.
ages 12 & up
ISBN 1-55652-249-5
208 pages, paper, $19.95

Bubble Monster and Other Science Fun... the Video!

As an aid to teachers, daycare providers, baby-sitters, and parents, this companion video makes *Bubble Monster and Other Science Fun* even easier to use. An engaging, fast-paced look at why to do *Bubble Monster* activities, when to do *Bubble Monster* activities, and how to do *Bubble Monster* activities. Whether used as a training tool for individuals, groups, or organizations, this video is an excellent supplement.

To order contact:
The YWCA of Annapolis and Anne Arundel County
1517 Ritchie Hwy., Ste. 201, Arnold, MD 21012
410-626-7800